# PROFILES IN CHARACTER

# PROFILES IN CHARACTER

## Jeb Bush and Brian Yablonski

Foundation for Florida's Future
Miami, Florida
1764

Library of Congress Catalog Card Number: 95-83319

ISBN: 0-9650912-0-1


Produced by K&N Bookworks
Book design by Michael Peterson

10  9  8  7  6  5  4  3  2  1

*To my wife, Columba, and my children, George, Noelle, Jeb; to my parents, who are my profiles in character, and to God, whose divine and guiding light is the ultimate means to virtue.*

—JEB BUSH

*To my wife, Kimberley, my parents, Steven and Donna, and my brother, Douglas, for their guidance and support in facing once and future challenges.*

—BRIAN YABLONSKI

# Preface

THE INSPIRATION FOR this book came in 1993, when William J. Bennett, the former U.S. secretary of education and drug czar, first published a report he called *The Index of Leading Cultural Indicators*. Today, most people across the nation are familiar with Bennett because of his best-selling book *The Book of Virtues*. However, before he pulled together his compilation of stories on virtue, Bennett published a paper and then a book of charts and graphs that detailed the decline of our civil society. *The Index of Leading Cultural Indicators* was based on the U.S. Census Bureau's Index of Leading Economic Indicators, eleven factors that together provide an accurate reading of our nation's economy. The only twist to Bennett's *Index* was that it featured indicators assessing the nation's social rather than economic condition. Bennett studied thirty-year trends in areas such as crime, out of wedlock births, divorce, scholastic achievement, child poverty and movie attendance. The results were not pretty.

In this book, we have tried to some extent to replicate and expand on this *Index*. Our initial goal was always to track the cultural and moral condition of the State of Florida for a period of time, starting, when we could, in the 1960s during the era of the Great Society. The book you are about to read is like a statewide visit to the doctor's office. We look at the symptoms of the disease known commonly as our ailing civil society, the cause of the symptoms and what treatment has been applied to date. As in Bennett's book, the factors that we review are called cultural indicators.

Most of our empirical evidence begins in Chapter Three and is dedicated to crime, poverty, education, teen suicide, personal responsibility and other indicators that reflect our common culture in a state of decline. But we also graph the decline of the traditional family unit and community by looking at out of wedlock births, divorce and the vitality of churches and synagogues and other civic organizations. It has often been said that families and communities are the first and original departments of health, education and welfare. Edmund Burke called them the "little platoons," and so do we when we look at their condition in Chapter Four. Finally, in Chapter Five, we present indicators reflecting the enormous growth of government that has occurred during the decades that all of this other bad stuff has been happening in Florida. Clearly, government is not the antidote to most of our problems.

Our book could have ended there. Somewhere in the midst of researching these astoundingly discouraging indicators, however, we found that there were some incredible people in Florida who were working hard and succeeding at reversing the seemingly irreversible. We looked back through the history of character and virtue and seized upon a classic Aristotelian theory. It is a remedy so rudimentary that it is like Mom prescribing chicken soup and tender loving care for a cold. Just as

Aristotle believed we became virtuous by practicing virtuous acts, so too it follows that we can learn something about good character through the stories of men and women of good character. Thus began the expansion of this project into what is now *Profiles in Character.*

Because any movement to reverse our cultural indicators will come only from individual effort and not government, we include the stories of fourteen true Florida role models. Most of them are Floridians whose names will rarely appear in a newspaper or whose good character is seldom publicly acknowledged. Lincoln would have called them "the better angels of our nature." We call them "profiles in character." They are not celebrities or pop icons but parents, neighbors and co-workers. These people are us. Each profile reflects some particular aspect of character that will be necessary for each of us to embrace to fulfill our Founding Fathers' vision of self-government in a free democracy. Their stories are meant to inspire and guide.

The good news is that finding these profiles in character in Florida was not difficult. There were many, many people whom we could have written about in this book. When we sent the word out, we received a number of excellent nominations for our profiles in character. It was our hope to obtain somewhat of a regional, racial, gender and generational balance to show these role models in all walks of life. Then we marshaled a small army of volunteers from all over the state to help us with the interviews and stories. Many of these volunteers were so inspired by the subjects they were interviewing that they threw themselves into their task, some choosing to get personally involved in their profiles' program. That is precisely what *Profiles in Character* is all about—directing us to the people who embody self-government through good character and inspiring us to emulate them.

Throughout this book you will notice that as coauthors we use the pronoun "we" to reflect our common thoughts and ideas. However, often the passages turn to the first person and the pronoun "I" is used, especially when recounting a story or an event. It should be assumed that when "I" is used in the first person that it is in Jeb's voice.

We hope that this book, while providing hard and sobering insight as to the depth of Florida's social problems, will inspire the readers to make more of a difference in their family lives and the life of their community. As Ralph Waldo Emerson once stated, "What lies behind us and what lies before us is nothing compared to that what lies within us." Our experience writing this book has taught us that we still have a great distance to go to live lives of good character. It is a journey we wish to take and we hope you will too so that we can pave a better future for our children and grandchildren.

—*Jeb Bush and Brian Yablonski*
*November 1995*

# Foreword
## by William J. Bennett

IN THE LAST decade of this American century, an important consensus has emerged: During the last thirty
years American society has experienced an astonishing
degree of social regression. I say "important consensus"
because recognition is often a precondition for
renewal. To borrow from a previous job I held in government, the recognition of the drug problem is the
first step toward an addict's recovery.

Now recognition is not everything, of course, but it is
something. And when it is conjoined with rigorous
analysis and intelligent commentary, you have the
makings of a valuable contribution to the public
debate. Which is precisely what Jeb Bush and Brian
Yablonski's fine book, *Profiles in Character*, is.

Floridians will be disturbed and alarmed by the
degree of cultural decay that has occurred in the nation
as a whole and in Florida in particular. Indeed, the
forces of social decomposition have hit Florida very
hard during the last three decades—and they have
left terrible human carnage in their wake. Consider just
one indicator: crime. Florida now leads the nation both

in overall and violent crime rates. Since 1960, the number of crimes committed in Florida increased an astonishing 744 percent! Crime has become more common,
more violent, more unpredictable. Juvenile crime has
dramatically increased—and it has worsened in terms
of sheer brutality and randomness. During the last
twenty years, the juvenile arrest rate has grown twice as
fast as the rate of juvenile population.

But there is much more to this book than an analysis
of social trends. *Profiles in Character* includes a thoughtful
discussion about the importance of virtue, character
and civility in a free society. Its authors understand the
crucial role of democracy's civic associations and its
"little platoons." And they reject the notion of an ener-
vating "nanny state," which, as Margaret Thatcher once
said, takes too much from us in order to do too much
for us.

Another aspect of this book worth calling attention
to is its profiles of civic heroes. You will see *Profiles in
Character* is inspirational as well as empirical. It
recounts examples of individuals who have made
(often at considerable sacrifice) a positive impact on
the lives of their fellow citizens. Ultimately, then, this is
a hopeful and instructive book. When we find success,
after all, we should do our best to encourage imitation.
Example, it has been said, is the language of men. We
should look to those who speak it best. Some of them
are profiled in these pages.

These profiles are examples of extraordinary people,
and they deserve our praise. But the rest of us need
to remember something that tends to get obscured
these days: Cultural renewal depends, finally, on
individual citizens living better and more decent lives.

It does not require sainthood, moral perfection or even moral excellence. It does require that we take seriously what too many Americans have come to neglect: our basic commitments as parents, spouses, neighbors, citizens and people of faith.

Let me close with a personal note. When Jeb Bush asked me to write the foreword to *Profiles in Character*, I agreed to do so because I thought it was a worthy project. The other reason is that I confess to being a big Jeb Bush fan. He is an intelligent, principled, civilizing force on the American political scene. We will hear more, much more, from Jeb Bush in the future. But for now, he has turned his considerable talents and energies to organizations like the Foundation for Florida's Future and books like *Profiles in Character*. Floridians will be the beneficiaries of his good work. He deserves congratulations for this impressive contribution.

—*William J. Bennett*
*Washington, D.C.*

# *Acknowledgments*

W E ARE ETERNALLY grateful to the many persons who helped make *Profiles in Character* possible. Foremost, we would like to acknowledge the great work of our premier editor, Sally Harrell, for her meticulous reading and revising of each and every draft of each and every chapter we produced. We would also like to thank Jean Becker, whom we also coerced into reading our drafts and who always provided us with wise feedback and insight.

Our profile stories would not have been possible without the many profile correspondents who helped with the research and composition of these short stories of inspiration. They include: Gretchen S. Adent, Brett Doster, Sandy Faulkner, Tom Gilliam, Sally Harrell, Maria Capote Hochman, Fonda McGowan, Marsha Nippert, Todd Pressman, Justin Sayfie and Janet Westling.

Our copublishers are the true reason we were able to continue this project as a self-publishing effort. Without their support, we could not have gone forward. The copublishers are Carlos Alfonso, Alfonso Architects, Robert Gomez, RG Commercial, The Variable Annuity Life Insurance Co. and Davis Baldwin Insurance and Risk Management.

In addition, we had many volunteers help us with research. Specifically, we would like to acknowledge the hard work of two special ladies, Yanette M. Moyano and Maria Capote Hochman, who were with us from the start. Other persons who assisted in the research and production include Frank Jimenez, Angela Vazquez-Mendes, Kris Cook, Brewser Brown, Cory Tilley, Jonathan Hage, Greg Turbeville, Ronald Krongold, Ana Martin, Toni Cook, Kasia Biernacki, Kelly Horton, Gene McGee, Andrea Wonsch, Allen Higgenbotham and Rodrigo Martin. Thanks to each and every one of you.

We would also like to acknowledge the support of the leadership of the Foundation for Florida's Future, many of whom sent in excellent suggestions for our profile stories. Furthermore, our thanks to Colson, Hicks, Eidson, Colson & Matthews as well as The Codina Group for their support while we worked on this project.

Finally, a special thanks to Bill and Dixie Bogusky for their cover design and to Tory Klose and Joan B. Nagy of K&N Bookworks for teaching us how to write a book.

# *Contents*

# CHAPTER ONE

# *The Value of Virtue*

*"Virtues" refer to the universal standards of right that bind all of us despite our differences and diversity.*

*"Values" are a set of beliefs, opinions and preferences.*

*Values are not the same things as virtues.*

*"Character" is that quality in a person that causes him to abide by a standard of right.*

*"Culture" refers to the moral, behavioral and social characteristics specific to a civil society.*

THIS IS A book about the renewal of character and virtue—the things that make us good and the most basic building blocks for any civil society. And, lest we forget their importance here in Florida, this book is also a call to arms.

It is only fitting that our message begins with the most beloved of the Founding Fathers, George Washington. In 1796, upon his retirement from the presidency and after decades of presiding over the birth of a nation, an aging Washington presented his farewell address to the people of the United States. In the historical accounts of this address, it is little remembered that Washington dedicated a portion of his parting wisdom to the eternal preservation of virtue and morality in the American people. The father of our country offered this pearl of wisdom, to be borne through the ages: "It is substantially true, that virtue or morality is a necessary spring of popular government. . . . Who that is a sincere friend to it can look with indifference upon attempts to shake the foundations of the fabric?"[1]

For Washington and his Colonial contemporaries, the strength of democracy in America would always reside in the good character and virtue of the American people. For the sake of our nation's future, Washington cautioned against entertaining those things that would threaten our good character. Almost forty years after the general's farewell address, it is rumored that a young Frenchman named Alexis de Tocqueville remarked while visiting America that "America is great because she is good, and if America ever ceases to be good, America will cease to be great."[2]

The great political thinkers of centuries past remind us today, at a time when we sorely need to be reminded, that the strength of our civil society has always been and forever will be grounded on the truism that Americans *are* good people full of good intentions. And yet those thinkers' simple words may mean more to us now than ever before. The last thirty years in our society have been marred by a cultural decline unprecedented in our nation's history. Here in Florida, the many cultural indicators tracking crime, education, poverty, out of wedlock births and a plethora of other social problems show the symptoms of this illness in our own state culture. We are becoming a society less safe, less educated, less family oriented and less likely to believe in the American Dream. Three quarters of the American population believe that the United States is in moral and spiritual decline.[3] Have we ceased to produce good people, people of character, or is there something else accelerating our societal ills?

If we have not lost our goodness, then we have certainly done our best to delegate it. The cultural indicators show that during that same thirty-year period, not coincidentally the size and power of government at all levels have increased. That growth is primarily a reflection of our own willingness to abdicate responsibility for governing ourselves. In the meantime, the federal and state governments have made the most of this tacit mandate, expanding further into our family life and communities. It was not until government became fully entrenched in our lives, however, that we found out just how ill equipped it was to handle the multitude of social problems.

It is becoming more and more evident in our own lives, in our families and communities, that we must take on added responsibility for addressing our societal ills. If, as Washington and Tocqueville observed, our nation's strength resides in the goodness of the people, then we must seize on our strong character and virtue for social problem solving. This means recognizing that self-government is the best government. It means doing a better job of instilling character and virtue in our children and helping those institutions charged with this task. It means not getting bogged down in the current and unwinnable debate over values. That debate must be redefined in the context of virtues. Only then can we lessen the demands on our state and federal governments and take matters back into our own hands. *The betterment of society starts from the bottom up through virtuous individuals and families and communities, not from the top down through more government.* This is the message.

# Then and Now

We begin with a tale of two eras in Florida. The Florida of 1960 was a much different place from the Florida of today. Transportation and communication were limited over our great expanse of land. Our interstate highway system was nonexistent or incomplete. I-75, I-95 and I-10 were not the great ribbons of pavement we know today. In 1960, there was no I-75. I-10 and I-95 consisted of only small sections of highway near Jacksonville. The Florida Turnpike was not completed until 1964. We were less likely to ever leave the place where we were born.

Our local value systems were rock solid. Indeed, there was little change or diversity to disturb them. There was no Disney World, no Magic Kingdom, no Epcot, no Universal Studios. Orlando was still a sleepy farming and ranching community. Florida did not have a single professional football team, major league baseball team or NBA basketball franchise. Our government was still functioning under the 1885 version of our state constitution, which had yet to provide for a lieutenant governor. Our population was less than five million people. With the advent of affordable air-conditioning, native Floridians—or Crackers as they were called—began to see the first trickles of immigrants from the northeast and Midwest resettling on the Florida coasts. It was a sign of things to come. And with the obvious exception of race relations, it was a less complex time in Florida.

Florida in the 1990s has an entirely different face. The expansion of our transportation and communication infrastructures has accelerated the increase in the number of people moving to Florida. Regional, racial and ethnic diversity abounds. We now find northeasterners on the east coast, midwesterners on the west coast, Hispanics in the south, native Floridians and the military infrastructure predominant in the Panhandle and north Florida and retirees throughout the state. Our population now hovers around fourteen million people. Many of our cities are among the most populous in the nation. We have the Dolphins, the Buccaneers, the Jaguars, the Magic, the Heat, the Marlins, the Lightning, the Panthers and, soon, the Devil Rays. Tallahassee now has a semiprofessional hockey team. Our state is widely recognized for the activities of NASA. Major companies such as Ryder Corporation, Knight Ridder, W. R. Grace and Burger King have all made Florida the home of their national headquarters.

As more and more people come to Florida from all over the world to start their lives anew, full of enthusiasm and hope, we are reminded that our geography and diversity also inevitably contribute to the dissolution of once cohesive value systems. In 1949, V. O. Key, Jr., author of *Southern Politics in State and Nation*, observed that as a result of Florida's geography, its political structure is "an incredibly complex mélange of amorphous factions."[4] Today, our social structure can be characterized in much the same way. We must often remind ourselves that, as the crow flies, the distance from Miami to Pensacola is about the same as from Washington, D.C., to Boothbay Harbor, Maine. Naturally, Miamians can be as unfamiliar to people in Pensacola as beltway bureaucrats can be to lobstermen.

And yet we do not propose a return to "traditional values." Though life in Florida in the 1950s and early 1960s was in many ways simpler and more homogenous, there were many obvious problems with the "traditional value" system. African Americans and other minorities had fewer opportunities, and Florida experienced racial segregation as much as any other state in the South. We had our fair share of lunch-counter sit-ins and riots. Women also faced obstacles under the old system. Today, these groups are assets to our state and participate actively in Florida's society.

This growth and change have been good for Florida as they have provided Florida with the most precious resource of all: human capital. The movement of people into Florida has brought energy and economic opportunity to the state. No doubt the eyes of the nation will be watching as we adapt to this rapid change for it is true that in many ways we reflect what the rest of the country will look like in the future. Population groups that are growing on a national basis, such as the elderly and the Hispanic, are already firmly entrenched in Florida's social structure. Florida today is tackling tough problems that other more stable states will come to experience in time. How will an Indiana or an Iowa respond to the instability of diversity and change that will descend upon their states? Chances are they will look to us for the answers.

Now for the bad news. Growth and change are realities in Florida and yet Florida has not done as well as it should to respond to the human factor. No matter what the benefits attending these changes over the last three decades, there can be no dispute that growth and change have had a profound effect on our communities, families and problem-solving networks. Our population not only grows; it also churns. More people in; more people out. More people dying; more people being born. And through it all, we have struggled to get our footing in the sand as the waves of change roll in and out. The cultural indicators will show that our way of life has radically changed. Our families do not look like the families they once did, our neighborhoods do not function the same way they once used to and our social problems reflect a general movement away from individual responsibility.

Against this backdrop, we cannot help but feel some shaking of what George Washington called the "foundations of the fabric." Our social structure buckles. When we look to our children, we see the problems of juvenile crime, drug abuse, teen suicide and the poverty of an education. When we look to the adults, we see many of the same problems along with out of wedlock births, divorce, domestic violence, material gratification and excessive litigation. When we look to the government, we see increased spending with no correlation whatsoever to results, layered bureaucracies, less effective output, personal ambition, special interest and self-interest at the expense of the whole.

Our population is increasing at a fast rate, but our social problems are accelerating at an even faster rate. Consider some of the indicators. Since 1970, our state population has increased 100 percent. Yet during the same span of time, out of wedlock births have increased by almost 300 percent. Since 1971, Florida's juvenile violent crime arrest rate has risen by 364 percent. Since 1972, combined Scholastic Aptitude Test (SAT) scores in Florida have declined by 62 points. Since 1960, the total number of divorces have increased by 322 percent. And since 1966, the number of children in Florida relying on Aid to Families with Dependent Children (AFDC) benefits, the primary component of welfare, has jumped 333 percent. As a state, Florida ranks among the worst in the nation in terms of out of wedlock births (40th), juvenile violent crime rate (49th), high school dropouts (45th), high school graduation rates (47th), performance on SATs (45th), percentage of children living in poverty (46th) and percentage of single-parent families (45th).[5]

# A Return to Self-Government

More and more, our response has been to look to government at all levels for the answers to our evolving social regression, which has resulted in a much larger and less effective bureaucracy. Take social spending and government employment as indicators of this growth and you will find that government is increasing at a rate equal to or greater than the problems government is trying to solve. For example, while the number of children relying on AFDC has increased by 333 percent since

1966, the actual amount of money government expends on AFDC benefits has increased from $25 million to more than $1.1 billion—an increase of 4,336 percent! At the same time, SAT scores have been dropping, expenditures per pupil in our public school system have increased by 442 percent since 1972 and the number of educational staff in our public schools has increased by 229 percent since 1970. Since 1960, the number of full-time state and local government employees has increased by 287 percent while the population during that same period increased by 182 percent.

Our overreliance on government is measured not only quantitatively, but qualitatively as well. We have abdicated to government our responsibilities in increments not discernible to the naked eye. This surrender has been a slow process, not a cataclysmic change, and it has come at the expense of our families and communities. During the 1994 gubernatorial campaign, Lieutenant Governor Buddy MacKay told me and an audience at a trade convention in Tallahassee that government was the best means by which we have decided to organize ourselves to solve problems. His statement was reflective of a cult of government that has developed over the years. We often forget that the original purpose of democratic government was *to protect the rights of individuals and to provide for things we could not possibly provide for on our own.* Abraham Lincoln said it best when he wrote that the legitimate object of government is "to do for a community of people, whatever they need to have done, but can not do, at all, or can not, so well do, for themselves—in their separate, and individual capacities. In all that the people can individually do as well for themselves, government ought not to interfere."[6] As examples of things government *should* do, Lincoln listed maintaining roads and bridges, disposing of deceased men's property and providing for the helpless young. The function of government is not to solve all our problems. It cannot do so. Individual effort, as Lincoln reminded us, has and always will be the first source of problem solving.

When we look at the cultural indicators in this book and to our ever expanding government, we have to ask ourselves "Is government really making things better as it relates to our social ills?" Take only those issues that deal with the welfare of our children and families and see how well government has done over the last thirty years. During this time, government has assumed more and more responsibility for the welfare of our children and families. Social legislation in this area has included welfare, no-fault divorce, child protective services, the juvenile justice system, centralized education, government programs for child support, foster care and adoption. Yet the institutions that have evolved from this social legislation have presided over an increasing number of divorces and out of wedlock births. They have watched as AFDC benefits have become an attractive alternative to marriage. State regulations have made it more difficult for adoptions to occur. Child support enforcement has been a disaster. Parents have less and less say in the education of their children. Our foster care system is ill equipped and impersonal, and in some cases, child abuse hot lines have had the unintended result of making it more difficult for parents to discipline their children. On top of all this, the family is now taxed more than ever to pay for all the "benefits" listed above. With the average family in Florida paying close to 40 percent of its income to government at all levels in return for services that many times don't work or have the perverse effect of making things worse for us, it is no surprise that most of us think we are on the wrong track.

When it comes to government, one virtue we are in need of is temperance. More government or reinvented government will not make our cultural pathologies go away. We must recognize the limits of what government can do. Government in some senses is like a pitcher in baseball. The pitcher plays an essential role in any baseball game. The pitcher is relied upon for defense, to keep the other team from scoring runs. At the same time, we do not expect the pitcher to be a slugger. The pitcher is not expected to provide runs, just prevent them. We recognize the pitcher's limitations. Government, too, has a role to play. We can rely on it for certain things, but there are some things it cannot do so well. Government is good for defense, to prevent crime, to prevent traffic accidents, to prevent all-around chaos. Yet government does not play offense so well. It does not provide wealth, it does not provide happiness, it does not fuel the American Dream. We cannot expect government to be both the pitcher and the slugger. At the turn of the century, American statesman Elihu Root said as much of government when he remarked,

> [W]hen we see how much misery there is in the world and cry out against it, and when we see some things that government may do to mitigate it, we are apt to forget how little after all it's possible for any government to do, and to hold the particular government of the time and place to a standard of responsibility which no government can possibly meet.[7]

Root's point was that we need to lessen the demands on government so that it can do well the things it does best. We must let it play defense. This means we have to look inward at ourselves rather than outward for the answers to our cultural problems. We must relearn the art of self-government—that is, we must embrace the knowledge that our own individual acts and behavior can have a profound effect on the culture of this state. Which brings us to the true purpose of this book: *to show that self-government can be achieved only by elevating character and virtue to the forefront of our lives.*

# Character and Virtue

For thousands of years, great thinkers, theologians and statesmen have written and agreed on the subject of virtue and its importance to society. Most have agreed that the cultivation of virtues in an individual makes him or her a good person, a respected citizen, a responsible parent. In a society full of virtuous people, there is an understanding of the common good and a high regard for the rights of others. The ancient Greeks were among the first to emphasize the necessity of good character. Aristotle defined moral virtue as a "state of character concerned with choice, lying in a mean."[8] It sounds confusing but for Aristotle, virtues were a compromise, a conscious decision between two extremes of feelings. For example, courage as a virtue involved a choice between cowardice and rashness. Similarly, temperance as a virtue involved a choice between self-indulgence and insensibility. A person of questionable character would be one who had lost or had never developed the ability to choose the mean.

In the twentieth century, one of the foremost modern scholars on the subject of cultivating virtues, social scientist James Q. Wilson, has written that having good character means at least two things: empathy and self-control.[9] Empathy is the ability to take into account the rights, needs and feelings of others. Self-control is exercising restraint over one's impulses, or deferring gratification or being more concerned with the long-term impact of conduct than with the here and now. The Greeks would have agreed with Wilson, since being empathic and practicing self-control means making choices that take into consideration the effects our behavior will have on others. Character, therefore, is of primary importance because it determines whether individuals will be selfish or selfless. In the final analysis, many of our cultural pathologies are a simple reflection of poor character, of being selfish instead of selfless.

But how do we ensure a healthy supply of selfless citizens? How do we go about cultivating virtue and developing persons of strong character from this generation to the next? For those who studied virtue, good character was not something inherited by birth or a gift of nature. Rather, character was an acquired skill, taught and fine-tuned by habit and practice. Aristotle wrote that "the things we have to learn before we can do them, we learn by doing them, men become builders by building and lyre players by playing the lyre; so too we become just by doing just acts, temperate by doing temperate acts, brave by doing brave acts."[10] Furthermore, most of the ancient and classical philosophers agreed that good character was something we begin cultivating early in our lives. It was generally thought then, and still holds true today, that we are best exposed to and influenced by character-forming institutions when we are young. It is when we are in our youth that we first develop the germ of character.

Before he passed away, former Speaker of the House Tip O'Neill wrote a book that included many of his favorite experiences and insights. In the book, he retold a wonderful story about a legislator who had been on the road for a month, had finally returned home and was reading through all the back copies of the local papers:

> His son came in and asked his dad to go outside and play catch. No, the father said, he had to read the papers. Five minutes later the kid was back, pestering his dad.
>
> "Look," the father said, "I want you to do something for me." And with that he took a map of the world, which happened to be in one of the papers, tore it in half, then quarters, then eighths and finally into sixteenths.
>
> "Now take this out in the kitchen and put it back together," he instructed.
>
> The kid was back in two minutes with the map assembled correctly.
>
> "My, I'm impressed," said the dad. "There are a hundred twenty countries in the world and you know them all."
>
> "Well, Dad," said the lad, "there was a boy's picture on the other side of the map and I just fitted it together."
>
> The moral of the story is: Put the youngster together right and the world will take care of itself.[11]

Herein lies a big problem with our ability to develop character and virtue. Our cultural indicators show something more than just increasing problems with crime, education, welfare and bigger government. The indicators show that those character-forming institutions traditionally charged with putting the youngster together right have experienced substantial disintegration of their own.

The moral education of our children has customarily been left in the hands of parents, the extended family, the neighborhood, the school, the church or synagogue and to some extent other civic associations. Yet when we look to the condition of each of these institutions, it is no wonder we hear more and more about gang violence, teen suicide, young girls giving birth and declining performance in our public schools. Our ailing children are simply a result of our ailing social institutions, families and communities.

Take each of these character-building institutions one by one and anyone can see the myriad problems needed to be overcome before we can truly be effective advocates of character and virtue. Today, parents and families are threatened by divorce and out of wedlock births. The neighborhood, once the paragon of the community, is no longer a warm familiar place but instead a gated enclave for the well-to-do or a war zone for the low income—both of which are cold and impersonal and weary of crime. As for public education, too many kids now leave our schools ill prepared for the challenges that lie ahead. Our schools have become receptacles of social experimentation, where teaching the basics is only one part of a menu of services provided. Our teachers have no choice but to join unions so that when they put a consoling arm around a child, they know they will be protected in a lawsuit by insurance that they would otherwise have to pay for themselves. Polls show that attendance is down in our churches, and religion is having less of an impact on people's lives. Our civic associations, formed with the intention of helping those in need, must now compete with government programs that require much less of the people they are helping. Unlike our traditional civic associations, government provides a lot of carrot but little concern for the stick.

## Virtues and Values and the Third Way

Many of the problems with our character-forming institutions go much deeper than simple surrenders to government. *They go to our losing the language of virtue*, to our inability to describe somebody as being virtuous in the context of goodness rather than in the context of chastity. Over the last few years, there has been a lot of talk about values but little discussion of virtues, which is almost entirely a language defect. What does it mean to have values and what does it mean to be virtuous? Do many of us know the difference? Our moral language problems reflect the difficulty we face every day in determining which set of moral standards guides our conduct and that of our children. We are finding that our complex and diverse society no longer functions under a uniform set of moral principles, but under competing personal and group value systems.

Values have replaced virtues as our moral lighthouses, and there are many different value systems present in our culture. Our character-building institutions have bought into the idea that we have to recognize all kinds of value systems and, instead of providing us guidance, now provide us with the tools to justify a wide variety of deviant behaviors. In other words, they do not teach our children right from wrong, but rather how to make informed choices. As one prison chaplain recently observed, our young children need direction, not choices. If we give them the proper direction, the principles by which to live their lives, then in the long run they will be more likely to make the right choices.[12]

We must become more *virtue* oriented and less *value* oriented. This is the third way to social problem solving. It recognizes that the first way, through traditional values, is not always good. It recognizes that the second way, through modern values, is not always effective, either. What this third way seeks to do is to renew character and virtue in the context of today's modern and changed society. If we moved the public debate to one about character and virtues rather than values and value systems, then we would see that there is no debate at all. People of any value system can agree on the importance of character and virtues. It is the only social solution that seeks a common ground. It is the only solution that allows the most devout liberal and the most fervent conservative to come eyeball to eyeball and agree.

This is because virtues and values are not the same thing. Tocqueville explained the distinction between virtues and values in his great work *Democracy in America.* He said that in judging the actions of men, public opinion generally employs two different standards: one relies on "simple notions of right and wrong, which are common to all the world" and the other assesses men "in accordance with some very exotic notions peculiar to one age and country. It often happens that the two standards differ; sometimes they conflict, but they never either completely coincide or completely oust each other."[13] Our problem is we have focused too hard and too long on the second standard: values.

The first standards of behavior—those moral absolutes common to all the world—may rightly be called virtues. They are standards of behavior that are fixed and firm in any civilized society. Who would argue that fortitude, prudence, justice, temperance, discipline, work, responsibility, honesty, honor and compassion are not good things? Listen to William Bennett: "Teaching virtue to our children need not be a controversial undertaking. Forming good character in young people does not mean having to instruct them on thorny issues like abortion, creationism, homosexuality, or euthanasia to name just a few.... [P]eople of good character are not all going to come down on the same side of difficult political and social issues. Good people— people of character—can be conservative, and good people can be liberal."[14] Virtues are agreed-upon standards of right and wrong.

Values, on the other hand, refer to a system of beliefs, opinions and preferences possessed by certain persons or groups. Values may be thought of best as a position. Even Nazis and the worst street gangs have values. Since values focus on a set of beliefs near and dear to ourselves, they have the tendency to accentuate our differences. We place a great deal of importance on our value systems and do not tread lightly when they are threatened. Recently, certain kinds of values have been labeled "traditional values" or "family values." At one point, our society generally agreed on these traditional values. Then something happened. Beginning with the social revolution of the 1960s, as a result of or in step with our social and public policy, we began to judge some of these more traditional values as antiquated. The traditional values were replaced by other, more contemporary values. Unlike thirty years ago, higher value is now placed on things such as self-expression, individualism, self-realization and personal choice.

Over the last three decades, traditional and modern values have inevitably clashed. And, as the indicators bear out, the modern values often trumped those traditional values such as accountability, moderation, deferred gratification, civic participation and commitment to the nuclear family and children. We have all seen the value of personal choice warring against the value of commitment to the family and children, the value of self-realization conflicting with the value of deferred gratification. As these value systems continue to battle for the moral high ground in our society, they have had the effect of canceling each other out, leaving us to confront the consequences of moral neutrality. All kinds of values are now used to justify all kinds of behavior. We can now rationalize any conduct into being proper.

Gertrude Himmelfarb argues in her book *The De-Moralization of Society: From Victorian Virtues to Modern Values* that because of this "anything goes" condition we have come to experience a "prevailing spirit of relativism, which makes it difficult to pass any moral judgments or impose any moral conditions."[15] There is no black and white, right or wrong, normal or abnormal. It was somewhere in this climate of conflicting values and moral neutrality that we lost the language of virtue.

While public policy over the last three decades has focused more on recognizing the differences among groups of people and their competing value systems, it did little in the way of reinforcing the common bonds among all peoples—the moral absolutes that transcend politics, race and gender. At some point in this whole evolving process, we got lost in the blizzard of values and we stopped talking about virtues. Virtues were either lost in the debate or they were mischaracterized as values—subjective and relative, personal and specific to a particular person or group. At that point, the language of virtue was no longer fixed and certain. This transformation was the politically correct thing to do because it enabled us to defend and justify our own personal conduct and lifestyles as a "value," which could not be judged against any higher standard. James Q. Wilson has noted, "Many people have persuaded themselves that children will be harmed if they are told right from wrong; instead they should be encouraged to discuss the merits of moral alternatives.... Many people have persuaded themselves that it is wrong to judge the customs of another society since there are no standards apart from custom on which such judgments can rest."[16] This is the hornet's nest Dan Quayle reached into when he gave his now infamous Murphy Brown speech. Vice President

Quayle was trying to speak in a universal language of virtue. His seemingly noncontroversial statement was that fathers play an important role in their children's lives, and it is better to have both parents than only one. But the statement offended the moral senses of many people. Today, there can be no doubt that the routine virtue-ladened speeches of Washington, Jefferson and Lincoln would be met with heavy-handed criticism.

Recently, we conducted a simple, highly unscientific experiment designed to see how often we use the word "virtuous" in our popular culture. Searching many of Florida's major newspapers for the word "virtuous," you might be disappointed to know that we found only a few random cites used frequently out of context. For example, since 1989, *The Orlando Sentinel* used the word "virtuous" to describe somebody or something on only 92 occasions. That is, only a little more than once a month. The *St. Petersburg Times* has used the word "virtuous" only 140 times since 1987, or fewer than 1 time each month. In most cases, "virtuous" was merely a term used to describe a character in a movie, play or book or, sometimes, a person in an obituary— nonpeople and dead people. This is certainly not to say that the newspapers are not reporting on the good deeds of virtuous people. We just aren't calling them virtuous anymore, further evidence that we have lost the language of virtue.

In a similar vein, the failure to use the language of virtue and our apparent inability to publicly pass moral judgments has led to the phenomenon Senator Daniel Patrick Moynihan calls "defining deviancy down."[17] Because of increased exposure to the strange or abnormal, we consciously lower the parameters of what we tolerate as acceptable behavior. Tabloid news has become the norm as we literally define deviant behavior down to normal behavior. Consider Senator Moynihan's account of the St. Valentine's Day Massacre in 1929. Most of us are familiar with the incident from our history textbooks. It involved four gangsters killing seven gangsters during Prohibition on Valentine's Day in Chicago. Senator Moynihan reminds us of the extensive coverage of this event. Then Senator Moynihan tells of a recent drug execution in New York City in which three people were slain. They were bound and gagged and shot in the backs of their heads. One woman managed to survive by hiding under a bed. Unlike the St. Valentine's Day Massacre, this story appeared only in the second section of *The New York Times*, at the bottom of the page. The contrast demonstrates not our approval of violent crime, but rather our trivialization of such crime, our growing accustomed to violent acts or other kinds of behavior that skirt the bounds of decency.

Another example. Imagine somebody in 1942 asking President Franklin Delano Roosevelt during a press conference whether he wore boxers or briefs. President Bill Clinton was asked this question on MTV in 1994. Many types of behavior no longer carry the stigmas they once did.

In Florida, we define deviancy down in our newspapers every day. Consider these headlines found in the remote reaches of our newspapers: MOM FATALLY STABS "MEAN" SON, 9, IN FRONT OF BROTHER (*The Miami Herald*, section B, page 1); DISMEMBERED BODY FOUND NEAR HIGHWAY (*The Tampa Tribune*, Florida/Metro section, page 4);

MAN KILLED DURING FIGHT ON VOLLEYBALL COURT; ANOTHER PLAYER IS HOSPITALIZED WITH GUNSHOT WOUNDS (*The Tampa Tribune*, Florida/Metro section, page 4). Crime is no longer outrageous to us. The FBI recently released statistics listing Ft. Lauderdale, Tampa and Miami as the three worst cities *in America* for crimes per capita, but even this made only the section B of *The Miami Herald*. We do not put the routine stories of heinous behavior on the front page anymore because they are no longer abnormal. Either that or we choose to deny their existence. Only the truly outrageous makes the front page. These essentially journalistic decisions should be taken as a warning. Have we in Florida reached the point where we have grown too indifferent to this abnormal behavior? Do we now treat our societal dysfunctions as if they were only part of a popular television show, surrealistic and out of reach? We are getting dangerously close to a time where, as Edmund Burke said, vice itself has lost much of its evil by losing all its grossness.

## The Bottom Line

Correcting our social pathologies will take time. Foremost, it will require a renewal of virtue and character and a rejuvenation of those institutions that teach virtue and character. We need to teach our children that there are universal rights and wrongs, that you can't spend your life explaining away or justifying deviant conduct. This means, then, that we must regain confidence in passing moral judgments, using the language of virtue and teaching virtue to our children. We hope we have turned the corner. To the surprise of many, William Bennett's *The Book of Virtues*, a collection of moral stories, was on *The New York Times* bestseller list for an amazing eighty-three weeks. We can only surmise that had Bennett titled his work *The Book of Family Values*, it would not have held such a coveted position for such a long period of time. In the summer of 1994, *Newsweek* ran an exposé on virtue featuring "The Virtuecrats" and a story entitled "What Is Virtue?" Two of the more popular movies from the last couple of years are *Forrest Gump* and *Apollo 13*, both movies about virtues, goodness and perseverance. And recently the cover of *The Atlantic Monthly* proclaimed DAN QUAYLE WAS RIGHT. People are getting a little more comfortable talking about character and virtue.

Earlier we asked "Have we ceased to produce good people?" We have been back and forth all over this state and we are convinced Florida is not lacking in men and women of character. It is important that we begin to discuss virtue and character in the context of those who exhibit true virtue and character on a routine basis. We must elevate the people who are redefining our culture every day for the better for they are the profiles in character from whom we must learn.

Following their lead, we must each grab hold of some portion of the reins ourselves. We must make a conscious effort to practice even small acts of character and virtue. Are we respectful of our elders? Do we accept defeat and victory gracefully? Do we throw trash from cars? Do we refrain from using profanity? Do we show up on time for meetings? These are little things that may not seem like much, but cumulatively speak volumes to our societal problems.

Benjamin Franklin once wrote that "little strokes fell great oaks."[18] It is a motto we should all adopt. There can be no doubt that our everyday acts, our little strokes, can affect society positively. Let us assume that each of the 14 million Floridians gets 100 chances a day to do something positive for our culture. And let us assume that we on average get it right 60 out of 100 times. Now, what would happen if through a conscious effort we improved our daily score to 80 out of 100 times? The cumulative effect would be inspiring. Twenty more virtuous acts multiplied by 365 days a year, multiplied by 14 million is 102 billion more acts of honesty, integrity, compassion, civility, prudence and courage each year. Do you think, then, that the demands on government would lessen? Do you think more than one third of all Americans would believe that the American Dream was alive? Do you think that there would be more hope and less despair? Each person has his or her own proportionate role to play in society no matter what his or her background. Good character is important in all aspects of society. If we roll up our sleeves and do our part, the answers to our cultural problems will come.

# CHAPTER TWO

# The Character of a Culture

THERE IS MORE than one way to measure our cultural decline. In the chapters to follow, we present numbers and graphs that track the evolution of our cultural problems back to the 1960s and early 1970s and provide us with a quantitative guide for evaluating our culture. However, there is also a qualitative element to our cultural decline too difficult to measure by numbers. Like the mighty Wizard of Oz hidden away, working his controls, with a booming voice, this qualitative aspect of our culture cries out, "Do not look behind that curtain!" But we do. And when we look long and hard beyond the statistics, we find the character of our own culture—the collective mind-set and attitude of our citizenry that speaks volumes about the moral erosion in our society. The character of our culture is the human factor that defies any scientific analysis.

Over the last twenty to thirty years, the character of our own culture has changed significantly. There can be no doubt that these changes have had a profound effect on our social conduct and public policies, often causing or contributing to our increasing social pathologies. The key is to identify and address these changes to our overall character in order to improve ourselves and our society.

In our own experience writing this book, we concede it is a difficult thing to put into a few concise sentences the true essence of society's collective character. One is reminded of a remark made by U.S. Supreme Court Justice Potter Stewart, who freely admitted that he could not define pornography but wrote "I know it when I see it."[1] Similarly, we know something about the character of our society because we see our social problems played out every day, in our families and neighborhoods, in the newspapers and on television.

In this chapter, we will give some thoughts on the character of our culture and outline what needs to be done to reinvigorate society's collective character. We use this chapter to explore such abstract questions as: Have we become too excessive in our individualism? Do we still react to public or private shame as we once did? Do we seek to avoid accountability and responsibility for our own conduct? Do we place more of an emphasis on our own personal happiness than on goodness? Are we out of touch with and disengaged from our neighbors? Has there been a breakdown in civility in society? Each one of these questions is addressed in an essay. Through our efforts to answer all of these questions, we hope to shed some light on many of our cultural problems—if not the root causes, then the root solutions.

# Our Individualism

The character of our culture begins with our strong tradition of individualism. There was a time when Americans were revered for their rugged individualism. The term referred to an American society based on the concept that all values, rights and duties originate in the individual. It meant that an individual in America could generally rise on her merits regardless of ethnicity, religion or upbringing. Though our nation's history is checkered with obvious exceptions, we were still far more advanced than most countries of the world in this respect. Furthermore, "rugged individualism" stood for the proposition that individual rights had primacy in American society. Our forefathers dissolved all bonds with England to secure the right to life, liberty and the pursuit of happiness as well as a right to free speech, a right to bear arms and a right to worship as one chose—all rights to be exercised by the individual. Our individualism is one of the few in the world that is codified in the national constitution—the Bill of Rights. Many of the most impassioned conflicts in our nation's history have revolved around these individual rights—slavery, the right to vote and abortion.

Today, our individualism helps define the American Dream. We are all unique persons with differing ideas of success and failure. This in turn provides Americans with a creativity and ambition unparalleled throughout the world. Individualism, fertilized by the nutrients of freedom, is what leads a person to think that she has just as much of a chance to succeed as her neighbor. It is what has led generations of parents to say of their children, "Just wait and see. Little Susie will be president of the United States one day."

Not many countries of the world can emulate this style of individualism. It is special because it has traditionally been tempered by responsibility and a respect for the common good. There was a time not so long ago when we were free to pursue the American Dream as individuals, but we were also held accountable for the far-reaching effects of our behavior. We recognized that our individualism needed to be practiced selflessly to benefit society. Practiced outside the bounds of common decency or practiced without concern for others' rights, individualism was reproached. In this sense, American individualism has been exercised within the context of the whole, not at the expense of the whole. Historically, we have done a fine job of taking many distinct peoples and many disparate views and forming a united country. The people have always retained their uniqueness within the greater whole, but there has always been a greater whole to which we proudly and confidently belonged, a greater whole with goals that were noble and important—freedom, democracy.

But today, this traditional notion of individualism is dying. It is gradually being replaced by a new type of individualism—"pure individualism." Many have called it hyperindividualism. Over the last three decades, our society has served as a midwife to the birth of an individualism practiced outside the context of the common good, an individualism where people are unfettered by duties, an individualism characterized by freedom from responsibility. Self-expression, self-realization, self-gratification, self-esteem and self-promotion are the values that define it.

Few can doubt that many of our cultural problems arise out of this unchecked individualism. It is individualism that has turned its back on virtue. Today, with all of our cultural problems—crime, poverty, suicide, poor education—it is not hard to recognize that without some sense of a greater whole (the whole being the family, the neighborhood, the community) individualism, in fact, causes a weakness in the character of our culture. It damages our ability to empathize, to exercise self-control and to give selflessly, the very definition of strong character.

In writing about America, Tocqueville mentioned an informal doctrine unique to this country called "self-interest properly understood." He detected a difference between Americans and Europeans when it came to helping their fellowman. Europeans helped their fellowman because they thought it the right thing to do while Americans helped their fellowman because they thought it the best thing to do, not only for society but for themselves. Tocqueville explained that "American moralists do not pretend that one must sacrifice himself for his fellow man because it is a fine thing to do so. But they boldly assert that such sacrifice is as necessary for the man who makes it as for the beneficiaries."[2] Americans understood that it was in each person's self-interest to be good. Being good to others was a way to instill character in ourselves and to ensure the virtuous acts would be reciprocated. "Self-interest properly understood" was the strongest guarantee against ourselves. This doctrine made individualism a strength of our national character. Americans properly understood the role of individualism and community in society. Tocqueville eloquently explained that "*the doctrine of self-interest properly understood does not inspire great sacrifices, but every day it prompts some small ones; by itself it cannot make a man virtuous, but its discipline shapes a lot of orderly, temperate, moderate, careful, and self-controlled citizens. If it does not lead the will directly to virtue, it establishes habits which unconsciously turn it that way."*[3]

For the most part, changes in our cultural character over the last few decades have involved a redefinition of the word "self"—a movement away from our nineteenth-century understanding of "self." The values prominent in today's society, which include self-gratification, self-expression, self-realization, self-promotion and self-esteem, do not impart the same sentiments as the "self" used in "self-control," "self-discipline" and "self-interest properly understood." The former group of values are "selfs" that aspire to be free from responsibility to others. They are narcissistic. The latter group are components of virtue.

Florida is fraught with examples, but the one that seemed to best capture the essence of the narcissistic "selfs" was the story of a particular forty-nine-year-old law student at Florida State University. The woman was an excellent student. She was in the top 10 percent of her class, awarded a position on the coveted law review and had a promising legal career ahead of her. She appeared to have a stable family life. She had been married for twenty-six years and had one fifteen-year-old son. In her spare time, she painted china dolls.

In the winter of 1995, the woman was working as a research assistant for one of her law school professors. While cleaning out a desk, she found a computer disk that contained exam questions for one of her classes. The woman made copies of the exam questions.

The law school secretary assigned to type the exam questions found out about the transgression. Furthermore, the woman had not only copied the exam questions but had also called the secretary to inquire which of the questions were going to appear on the exam. It was not long before the woman was notified that she was being charged with honor code violations.

Fearing her promising legal career was coming to an end, the woman decided to take drastic measures. She called an acquaintance in the Florida Keys and asked to be put in contact with a hit man. The person she was put in touch with contacted Florida law enforcement officials and agreed to cooperate. When the woman called the hit man, she offered him a thousand dollars to kill the law school secretary. She told the hit man that she needed to take the secretary "out of the picture," otherwise she would lose her whole law career. During the phone call, the woman told the hit man where he could find the secretary and said, "It must look like a total accident.... I'm talking about a situation like there's one car accident; the car leaves the road and hits a tree or whatever, and the driver has a broken neck."[4]

As if this was not enough, the story gets even more bizarre. Sinking faster and faster, the woman made a followup call to the hit man to amend her plans. Not only did she want the law school secretary murdered, but she also wanted her husband of twenty-six years killed! She told the hit man that with his life insurance money, she could pay for both hits and eliminate two problems—her cheating and her husband's sharing in her earnings after she became a lawyer. These phone conversations were taped by law enforcement officials and the woman was arrested for solicitation to commit murder. In the fall of 1995, she pleaded no contest and was sentenced to four years in prison.

This story is strange and extreme, indeed. However, it is a real-life story of self-realization and of freedom from responsibility. We all know persons who have been so driven by personal goals that they have been willing to sacrifice, in a figurative way, people they know or love. This is nothing new to our history. However, in a moral climate that encourages this type of hyperindividualism, these kinds of incidents are bound to happen with more frequency and in parts of our state, in communities and neighborhoods, where we might not think this kind of thing could happen.

The evolution of individualism and the divorce of the "self" from the whole may be the single most significant qualitative change in our culture, leading to the worsening of our social problems, an overreliance on government and the breakdown of the family and community. The character of our culture needs to be bolstered by promoting that which contemplates something more in society than just ourselves. *To restore the balance between the individual and the community is the rub.* As Edward Gibbons reminded us, Athens, the birthplace of democracy, fell because Athenians wanted society to give them more than they were willing to give to society. According to Gibbons, when the freedom the Athenians were seeking became freedom from responsibility, then Athens ceased to be free.[5]

Character curtails the drive for freedom from responsibility. It prevents the simple lover of liberty from becoming a libertine. What do we need to do to restore the strong character of our people? Read on.

# The Restoration of Shame

When Aristotle wrote his treatise on ethics, he identi-
fied many particular virtues important in his time. His
list of virtues included courage, temperance, justice and
other basic virtues still considered important today. He
also created a special category of virtue, which he called
"quasi virtues." In it he placed shame.

It is hard for us today to imagine that at one time this
emotion was a virtue, or at least a quasi virtue. But this
should come as no surprise. Shame has always been an
important mechanism for exercising self-control. When
a person feels shame, it is out of a concern for what his
or her peers think. In a classical sense, it is a "kind of
fear of dishonour."[6] Whether those peers are parents,
neighbors, fellow students, co-workers or even somebody we don't know so well, it is important that there
be a person out there who will cause us to feel some
sense of remorse for particular types of behavior. When
we feel shame, it is because we belong to a community
or group that we care about. Shame is one of the great
regulators of conduct. At times, it regulates behavior
that laws do not. Other times, it is the force that drives
us to comply with laws.

But shame is not something that comes automatically.
It requires negative reinforcement by those persons in
society closest to our children. These people in their
public and private lives need to do all they can to
express displeasure with irresponsible behavior, not
coddle or reward.

In our culture today, however, there is very little "fear
of dishonour." One of the reasons more young women
are giving birth out of wedlock and more young men

are walking away from their paternal obligations is that there is no longer a stigma attached to this behavior, no reason to feel shame. Many of these young women and young men look around and see their friends engaged in the same irresponsible conduct. Their parents and neighbors have become ineffective at attaching some sense of ridicule to this behavior. There was a time when neighbors and communities would frown on out of wedlock births and when public condemnation was enough of a stimulus for one to be careful. Infamous shotgun weddings and Nathaniel Hawthorne's *Scarlet Letter* are reminders that public condemnation of irresponsible sexual behavior has strong historical roots.

Shame also has historical underpinnings in the way we treated criminals. Pillories and public dunkings in Colonial times were common. In more recent times, the return of chain gangs exemplifies the use of shame in criminal justice. But much of today's criminal justice system seems to be lacking in humiliation. Juvenile offenders wear their detention as a badge of bravery among their friends. I could not imagine what my parents would have done to me if I had been arrested when I was a teenager, but apparently that kind of threat no longer carries the weight it once did. Kids are more concerned with what their peers think. That may be a reason why street gangs are displacing families. In the context of present-day society we may need to make kids feel shame before their friends rather than their family. *The Miami Herald* columnist Robert Steinback has a good idea. He suggests dressing these juvenile offenders in frilly pink jumpsuits and making them sweep the streets of their own neighborhoods! Would these kids be so cavalier then?

It's not just our inner city streets that are in dire need of some sense of shame. We have also lost shame in our schools, too. Specifically, there is little shame in poor academic performance or classroom misconduct. We now see many students who do not care if the teacher yells at them or if their test results are less than stellar. In many of Florida's largest school districts, there is little that the teacher can do to make students feel some sense of shame. In some school districts, such as Walton County, one of the oldest forms of shame, corporal punishment, is alive and well, and despite protests by some parents and Florida's PTAs, the students in Walton have actually found that this doling out of shame is very effective. The students of these schools will tell you, as will anybody who experienced corporal punishment in school, that it is not the brief spanking that hurts but the accompanying shame. A senior vale-dictorian of one high school in Walton County told a reporter, "We feel ashamed when it happens to us, but when you're in that classroom and you want to learn and somebody else won't let you learn, well, they are dealt with."[7] To date, Walton County has never experienced a shooting at any of its schools.

Another example of how we have come to devalue shame in society is in our welfare system. Marvin Olasky, in his excellent book *The Tragedy of American Compassion*, shows that before the Great Society of the 1960s, one of the reasons the welfare rolls remained relatively low was because "[a] sense of shame was relied upon to make people reluctant to accept 'the dole' unless absolutely necessary."[8] As a result, in the mid-1960s, only half of those eligible for welfare payments were taking them and many enrolled would refuse to take the maximum allowance. People shined shoes and found other ways to bring in money that by today's standards would be considered shameful. However, by the late 1960s and early 1970s, the stigma of receiving welfare had been lost by an administration that encouraged receipt of welfare. The rolls exploded as a much higher percentage of those who were eligible suddenly thought it less shameful to take advantage of the benefits rather than employ themselves in a job requiring hard work, such as shining shoes or sweeping floors.[9] For many it is more shameful to work than to take public assistance—that is how backward shame has become!

In Florida, our need to restore shame is evident at the higher end of the socioeconomic ladder as well. Our bankruptcy and homestead laws foster irresponsible financial behavior without a corresponding stigma. A person in Florida who has frivolously piled up enormous debts or engaged in all kinds of risky financial activities can file for bankruptcy and wipe the slate clean. In the meantime, that same person can keep assets, such as a spectacular mansion, through the homestead and other exemptions that can total millions of dollars. A businessperson in Florida may go through bankruptcy a number of times in his or her life without fear of dishonor. In fact, our laws are so shameless that many people from outside the state establish themselves in Florida merely because of our bankruptcy exemptions.

There needs to be a restoration of shame in our society and that restoration should be universal, not something used only to motivate the poor in the inner city. Similarly, the restoration of shame should be something more than just humiliation and something more than just physical, such as paddling. Shame works only when it instills a fear of disapproval. When I was growing up, a big motivator in my life was the fear of receiving my father's disapproval. It did not mean I had to be spanked or that I had to be humiliated in front of the family. All it took was for my dad to say, "Jeb, I am disappointed in you." That was enough of a blow and I never wanted to feel that way again. Today, in many families that may not be enough. The fear of disapproval needs to be taught by parents at an early age. Parents need to command the respect of their children by example; they need to practice character. I do not know if I would have had the same fear of my father's disapproval if he was not such an honorable and good man.

Society needs to relearn the art of public and private disapproval and how to make those who engage in undesirable behavior feel some sense of shame. We must be accountable to something more than just ourselves, and the restoration of shame and stigma may be society's way of restoring accountability. Shame helps to keep us virtuous by constantly forcing us to think before we act. As Edmund Burke wrote on this very subject, "While shame keeps its watch, virtue is not wholly extinguished in the heart."[10] Similarly, it has been noted that man's ability to blush truly distinguishes him from the animals.[11] To this end, bettering the character of our culture may ultimately depend on our ability to teach the next generation how to blush.

# The Restoration of Accountability and Responsibility

"The devil made me do it" is a familiar saying we have probably all used at some point in our lives to excuse our behavior. Avoiding accountability is nothing new to our culture and history. But what does distinguish the culture we live in today from the culture of yesterday is the enshrinement of our opposition to personal accountability and responsibility. Our society is becoming more and more a place where no one is guilty, nobody fails and everybody is a victim of some injustice in the world.

Today, people argue that the lazy are not responsible for their lack of success, that parents are not accountable for their children's misbehaving in school or dropping out altogether, that criminals should not be held accountable for their conduct because of their upbringing. The problem is not in our tendency to avoid accountability for some things, but in our tendency to now avoid accountability for all things. Our no-fault laws, the politics of victimization and the fear of failure and competition in our schools and businesses are all recent antiaccountability movements. As this blame game is played out in our culture, it is beginning to make headway into our political and legal institutions, leaving our children with the undeniable message that they, too, can avoid responsibility for the consequences of their actions.

## No-Fault Society

Consider our rising status as the great no-fault society. In the 1970s, the no-fault divorce reform movement swept through the country. No-fault divorce abolished defenses to divorce and liberalized the grounds for dissolution of a marriage. But no-fault divorce quickly became a tool for those who used the law not to escape physical or mental cruelty but to pursue career dreams and trade in their wives for something more appealing.

Auto insurance is no fault. In parts of the country, there is no-fault flood insurance, care of the federal government, for those who build houses on flood plains knowing that they will be bailed out when their home is destroyed in a flood. We have no-fault workers' compensation laws and no-fault firings, which ensure that employees laid off will receive healthy severance checks. There is even no-fault psychotherapy, where patients are told that the root of their misconduct is not themselves but some childhood trauma that they had no way of controlling. No fault is a concept that has also permeated our criminal justice system. Over the last three decades, the courts have permitted a number of no-fault defenses, such as insanity and sexual abuse, raised in the trial of the Menendez brothers. Now any criminal defendant can arm himself with an excuse from his past to exonerate a crime.

It seems that fewer and fewer people today know how to say the words "It is my fault." In such a society, who will be responsible for personal conduct, who will accept responsibility for a civil society in decline? If you cannot be blamed for the things you have done yourself—the way our children are, the way our public school systems are, the way our inner cities are—how can you be blamed for things that happen outside the sphere of the "self"? In a no-fault society, we will never be able to accept responsibility for society's ills and we are in grave danger of becoming a society that never feels compelled to correct them.

### The Politics of Victimization
Another manifestation of our evolving movement against personal accountability and responsibility is

the politics of victimization, which recognizes that being a victim of societal injustice often means being held to a different standard of accountability. It provides a person with an excuse for behavior and it is a way of securing something desirable by avoiding individual achievement. When people view themselves as victims, as part of some smaller oppressed group, they often see life in terms of "us against them," the oppressor against the oppressed. But often the oppressor is viewed as anybody not in the oppressed group. This victimization is reaching absurd levels. Look at how many criminals are the victims. Prisoner lawsuits are clogging our judicial system. We even consider a criminal's background before passing judgment. Was he abused? Was he poor? Were his parents drug addicts? Did he have an abnormal upbringing? All unfortunate circumstances, but no excuse for criminal behavior.

Since the 1960s, the politics of victimization has steadily intensified. People have gradually learned that being a victim gives rise to certain entitlements, benefits and preferences in society. These entitlements are bestowed with little or no corresponding responsibilities. The surest way to get something in today's society is to elevate one's status to that of the oppressed. Many of the modern victim movements, the gay rights movement, the feminist movement, the black empowerment movement and other movements based on social status or race have attempted to get people to view themselves as part of a smaller group deserving of something from society rather than viewing themselves as an integral part of a society in which they strive to make a contribution to the whole.

It gives us no comfort to know that society now organizes itself into blocks that engage in group thinking. These blocks are a logical progression of special interest groups with their own agendas for advancing themselves, agendas often based not on merit but on some immutable characteristic. It is a major deviation from the society envisioned by Dr. Martin Luther King, Jr., who would have had people judged by the content of their character and not by the color of their skin—or sexual preference or gender or ethnicity. Eventually, there will come a time in our culture when everybody will be able to claim some status as a victim of society, leaving few in society who will actually be considered the victimizers. Who, then, will be left to blame in a world in which it is victim against victim?

### The Fear of Failure and Competition

Finally, the last antiaccountability movement we would like to address is our growing aversion to failure and competition. Personal accountability means that you may sometimes succeed because of your actions and you may also fail because of your actions. But in today's changing culture there is a movement against taking responsibility for your failures. More often than not, this opposition to failure is fostered in our school systems. From kindergarten to the university system, the schools of our modern culture go far out of the way to ensure that nobody is distinguished, or undistinguished, for his failure to keep up with his classmates. Often this is done in the name of self-esteem. However, it has the marginalizing effect of teaching our children that they can do no wrong. This demeans those who work hard to see themselves only slightly distinguished from the problem children in the classroom. It is no way to teach accountability.

A story to illustrate this point comes from the 1994 gubernatorial campaign trail. While campaigning in Hernando County, I was invited to visit an elementary school. It was one of the newer schools in the county with very pleasant architecture and very pleasant landscaping. Indeed, everything was very pleasant. The day I was there, an awards ceremony was taking place for one of the grades. Several hundred kids were in attendance along with thirty to fifty parents. The idea was to reward the children who had done well as a way of inspiring the others to try harder and to motivate the hard-working ones to keep it up. It reminded me, or so I thought, of my own experiences in elementary school when the teachers used to put gold and silver stars on the tests of those who had done well. At that age, we all strived to do well so that we could show our parents the shiny gold star on our exams.

But as the ceremony in this particular elementary school continued, it became clear that something was different. All the children in the class were being called up individually to receive a certificate. How could *every* child be doing so well? I was sitting in the front and as each child came up, I looked at what the certificates said. Christie received one that said the Principal's List, which was the highest honor. Antoine got the Honor Roll certificate. Other certificates were for good reading. Finally, quite a few children received a certificate that said Bear's Club. I asked one of the teachers what the Bear's Club signified and was told that this basically meant the student had showed up. I asked the principal why every child had received an award. Why didn't the best students get specially recognized rather than just receiving a certificate like everybody else? He told me that it would not be good for the self-esteem of the rest of the kids to recognize only the achievers, and it was good for all the others to receive something, anything, even the mighty Bear's Club designation.

The story says a lot about our culture but it does not end in our elementary schools. This same self-esteem excuse is used today in a variety of forms at many of our institutes of higher learning. As discussed in the next chapter, the College Board is recentering the Scholastic Aptitude Test, resulting in higher test scores for all. Similarly, many of our graduate and professional schools these days function on an inflated grading curve. A grading curve means that a majority of students receive the arbitrarily designated grading curve grade. The grade upon which the curve is based is considered average in the class. Nothing too controversial so far. However, the surprise is when you hear what the grading curve grades are at some of the nation's most prestigious schools and how they have increased over the years. For some of these schools, the curve is set at a B+. That means anything below a B+ is considered below average. It is not that all the students are performing B+ work but that the teachers are required or that it is "strongly recommended" by a grading curve policy to artificially inflate the students' grades so that B+ is the average. Therefore, students in a class could be performing only C work, but because the grading curve is a B+, those students' grades will be bumped up to a grade of B+ or higher. We know of at least one graduate school in South Florida that within the last couple of years moved its grading curve from a C+ to a straight B. So, like Garrison

Keillor's Lake Wobegon children, all of our children are now above average.[12]

The justification for this high grading curve is apparently part self-esteem and part fear of competition. Educators today are as concerned with the psychological well-being of their students as they are with their intellectual success. A more practical justification is based on the realities of the business world. That is, in business, most employers hiring college graduates look to students' grades in evaluating their potential. Colleges and universities are often judged by where their alumni land in the marketplace. With these two factors combined, many schools in the upper echelon now inflate their grading curves so that their students will have an advantage in the job market. As other schools get wise to this grade inflation, they, too, inflate their grading curves, breeding a culture of perceived successes and abhorrence to failure.

Another example of this fear of failure and competition involves many of the law schools across our state. There, the opposition to competition and failure is present not only in the grading curve system but also in other forms of academic honors. One of the most coveted honors in any law school is to earn a place on law review, the premier legal periodical for the law school that is full of scholarly articles edited and often written by the brightest the school has to offer. Employers often use student membership on law review as a hiring threshold, with those job seekers who were on it holding a distinct advantage in the marketplace. Membership on law review is highly selective and based primarily on academic achievement in the first year of law school. At one time, membership was based solely on first-year grades, but as students complained about the unfairness of merit based on grades, law reviews began to offer an alternate way of gaining membership—a subjective writing competition. Soon the injustice of law review became so unbearable that law schools began to create more law reviews, or Bear's Club law reviews, if you will. While many schools still have the traditionally recognized law review, they also have many other specialized legal periodicals called law review for those students who did not make it onto the traditional review. Many schools have an international law review, an environmental law review, a sports and entertainment law review, a business law review, a public policy law review. The practical effect is that almost any student can now put "law review" on his or her résumé. Employers not familiar with the exact title of the premier law review at a particular law school can be easily hoodwinked into thinking the applicant before them was on *the* law review. Many law firms now disregard or place less emphasis on the law review designation on a résumé because, as one hiring partner in a national firm has said, "Anybody can say they were on law review." Again, it is an example of our schools' trying to level the talent pool when employers are trying to accomplish the exact opposite—finding out who is best qualified to serve their businesses.

Our no-fault society, the politics of victimization and our opposition to failure and competition are all signs that our culture needs to restore personal accountability and responsibility to some extent. These self-indulgent notions damage society's respect for merit and personal striving. We must not be afraid to take credit for both our successes and *our mistakes.* Character is often best built by taking responsibility for adversity rather than for success.

# Being Happy and Being Good

A number of months ago, Anthony Campolo, a Baptist minister from New Jersey, was in South Florida to discuss his work in inner city projects. In speaking to a Presbyterian congregation in Miami Shores, he touched on another facet of the character of our culture. He noted that parents today are more apt to be concerned about whether their children are feeling happy than whether their children are being good. Parents are willing to spend outrageous sums of money to buy their children the nicest toys, most stylish clothes, fancy cars, the best education, all in an effort to make them happy. But what do these parents do to make their children good? Being good and being happy are not the same thing.

Teaching a child to be happy without teaching her to be good only reinforces those "self" values that defeat the purpose of good character and virtue. A child preoccupied with being happy will become an adult preoccupied with pleasure seeking and instant gratification. Today society is bent on such slogans as JUST DO IT and IF IT FEELS GOOD, DO IT. These slogans speak to an urge to satisfy our own personal happiness rather than to a desire to achieve goodness.

In one of the more moving moments of his lecture, Campolo told the story of a friend of his who served as the president of a major seminary in the south. Everything was going great for this upwardly mobile educator until his wife became afflicted with Alzheimer's disease. Her condition deteriorated rapidly to the point where she could not even recognize her husband. Friends of his encouraged him to keep up with his duties at the school and to hire a nurse to take care of his wife. They encouraged him not to throw away his career. In the end, the educator resigned from his prestigious post to care for his wife full time, even though she did not know who he was. He told his friends he had made a vow for better or for worse and he intended to stick by it. For years, the educator looked after his ailing wife as she worsened and faded away. The educator was not happy but he *was* full of goodness. And that is the difference between being happy and being good. When the educator reached the crossroads, he chose goodness over happiness, responsibility over self-realization. We often wonder how many of us would choose to be good rather than happy under similar circumstances.

Similarly, Bill Galston was at the peak of his career when he resigned from his job to spend more time with his ten-year-old son, Ezra. Galston's job required him to work twelve hours a day and often on weekends. As a result, he would miss Ezra's Little League baseball games, and when he got home from work he would be so exhausted that the time spent with his son was lacking in quality. Things got so bad that Ezra began waking up at 6:00 A.M. just because he knew his dad would always be in the house then. Finally, Galston received a short letter from his son listing the ten-year-old's baseball achievements he had missed because of work: first winning run, first hit, first stolen base and on and on. At that point it became too much for Galston and he quit his job. The day he resigned, Bill Galston walked into the Oval Office and told his boss, President Clinton, "You can replace me. My son can't."[13] And so William Galston resigned from his senior White House position as domestic policy adviser to the president of the United States. Like the educator from Campolo's story, Galston stepped off the ladder of success by corporate or political standards but stepped onto a new ladder of success. This new ladder was guided by his ten-year-old son's standards.

So William Galston was a good man who could derive equal happiness by spending more time with his son. Being good, however, does not always mean sacrificing something important. Being good is about making the right decision at the right time. Deciding not to get high on drugs or alcohol, deciding not to engage in irresponsible sexual relations are decisions to defer pleasure and happiness. Being good is about teaching our children that at points in their lives where goodness and personal happiness conflict, goodness should win every time. Because we are human, goodness will not win out every time, but we should strive as hard as we can for a perfect record. We teach this to our children not by showering them with goodies but by showering them with examples of goodness.

# Restoration of Social Engagement

In 1995, Robert Putnam, a Harvard professor, conducted a study that showed too many of us who are bowlers are not members of bowling leagues. The study found that while the number of Americans bowling is up 10 percent, participation in bowling leagues is way down, as much as 40 percent since 1980.[14] The study was used to make a point: We are becoming a nation of atomized and socially disconnected individuals. We are too isolated from one another.

Character is based on interaction and socialization. It is often said that man is a social animal. Being in contact with, dealing with, spending time with other people is critical to the process that enables us to be more than just atomized individuals. By increasing our social interaction in our neighborhoods and communities, we develop a trust for, cooperation with and understanding of others. While we can be satisfied and happy in our own lives, social interaction allows us to feel compassion and responsibility for our neighbors and communities. It enables us to come together in society to address common problems or share common successes. That is the strength of democracy.

America has a proud tradition of civic and social engagement. Tocqueville was awed by our civic associations and noted that "Americans of all ages, all stations in life, and all types of disposition are forever forming associations."[15] He found that in America, we formed associations to found seminaries, build schools, distribute books, give festivals. Associations have customarily been important to accomplish that which needed to be done beyond the competence of one individual. The importance of these associations was their socializing effect. Tocqueville wrote, "Feelings and ideas are renewed, the heart enlarged, and the understanding developed only by the reciprocal action of men upon one another."[16]

*Our history teaches us that we have the capacity for self-*

*government only as long as we are socially connected to our fellowman.* Conversely, the less time we spend in physical contact with others, the less socialized we are—the less we understand our common concerns and endeavors. For many of us, however, social disconnection is easy and getting easier. Our preoccupation with individualism has weakened group life. How many of us really know our neighbors? How many of us have spent large portions of time in parts of our community where we do not live or work? America may be a melting pot but Americans generally dislike the company of others. Our privacy can make us all too comfortable.

Part of this has to do with our massive transportation, communication and technological transformations, which have provided us with the superhighway infrastructure, increased air travel, the information highway, Internet, VCRs and cable TV. While each has done many a good thing for society, each has had its own desocializing effect on us. Specifically, we are reminded of a sad story in the newspaper about an old man who passed away at a retirement facility. His family went to collect his belongings and found his room flush with gadgets and toys that had been bought through the Home Shopping Network or QVC. Apparently, the man did not have many friends and often spoke of being lonely. The only way he felt he could remedy this loneliness was by calling home shopping operators and spending many hours on the phone with them buying things.[17] Television afforded him the opportunity to have company without ever leaving his room, but added to a deepening sense of isolation. This story is not uncommon among many of the isolated and lonely elderly in our state.

At one time, our nation was characterized by the stability of our communities. Generally, we grew up in one community. It was the same place where we went to school, met our spouse, settled down and eventually raised a family. We knew many people in our community and were involved in different organizations—church group, Little League, PTA. We cared about our community because we knew everybody in it.

In the modern era, our ability to physically move has increased. Historically, the nation has experienced at least two great population movements—pioneers moving west and African Americans moving from the south to the north. Today, we are a much more mobile society without discernible population movements. We don't have massive population movements anymore because travel is quick, occasional and done without extended families or communities. As opportunities arise elsewhere, we can more easily pick up and go. Similarly, as problems arise in our communities, we can just as easily leave. For those who move often, it is difficult to develop ties to one community. The composition of whole neighborhoods can change in a few years. For a growing number of us, the place where we grew up is not where we now live. If we returned to the neighborhoods where we grew up, few of us would find familiar faces. Today, many more of us are far away from our immediate and extended families, families that are often splintered around the country. Sometimes, as with the old man in the retirement facility, this results in the impersonal care of loved ones by service providers. There is in our society a general lack of spatial connectedness.

In Florida, we feel this more than most other areas of

the country because our state is saturated with those who move here to start anew or to retire. As social scientist Charles Murray has observed, "We have become a nation of subdivisions and apartment blocks, places where people eat and sleep but too seldom live together as neighbors and copartners in making their little platoons work."[18] Dr. Murray's comment on the nation applies even more to the Sunshine State. So little continuity in our communities inevitably causes people to lose their interest in civic engagement, and there are fewer associations, fewer groups and less social activity that involves the whole community.

But our desocialization is not merely confined to the changes in our communities. Computers, video games, VCRs, Walkmans and other forms of entertainment have also worked to socially disconnect us. Instead of playing in a neighborhood game of touch football after school, children play Mortal Kombat and other computer games. Adults may be no better. The arrival of the modem has meant hours spent in front of a personal computer, online, surfing the Internet. It is far too easy for us to address a concern at work or in our personal lives via e-mail instead of by picking up the telephone or going to see a person. While technology has its obvious benefits, communicating with one another through a computer has its downfalls. We don't see the person, we don't hear a voice, we can't feel inflections or see expressions. Spats arise between people because something written in jest and sent by e-mail is read seriously—the person at the other end of the e-mail message lacked the human contact that would have easily told him he was being kidded or teased. Not only do we lose the human contact with the persons we are communicating with but also the time spent online or tuning out with your Walkman is time spent away from your spouse, your children, your neighbor. We, too, like our children, are becoming socially disconnected from our fellowman.

Clifford Stoll is a physicist and astronomer who became a cyberspace celebrity in 1988 when as a computer system manager for the government at the Lawrence Livermore Laboratory he uncovered a German-based spy ring operating over the Internet. In his latest book, *Silicon Snake Oil*, Stoll critiques the usefulness of computers and the information highway. Stoll wonders if the information highway, like its predecessor the superhighway, has not moved us further apart instead of bringing us closer together. He points out that computers, with their electronic games and volumes of data banks, have the tendency to isolate us from one another by consuming so much of our time and by removing us from human contact. He writes that "during the week you spent on-line, you could have planted a tomato garden, volunteered at a hospital, spoken with your child's teacher, and taught the kid down the block how to shag fly balls."[19] We spend too much time downloading gobs of useless information and this is becoming a serious problem for our culture because, in Stoll's words, "You cannot download your ability to get along with someone else."[20]

The social canyons created by rushing rivers of technology and modernization must be bridged. But we must be careful not to undo the good things these rivers have brought us. In the first chapter, we discussed the third way—our need to renew character and virtue in the context of today's modern and changed society.

The third way works in this setting as well. We must reengage ourselves in our social settings, in our neighborhoods and communities, but do so in a way that acknowledges the advances made by our society. While we should never turn back the clock on our technological advances, we should be aware of their potential effects—both bad and good. We should practice our technology in the context of character and virtue. Use it for the benefit of mankind, not to stimulate isolated pleasure. We must continue our technological revolution but we cannot use it as a substitute for social interaction. For a society moving deeper into the computer age, we need to remember that our ability to get along with others is what good character is all about.

# Restoration of Civility

Sometimes, a little hypocrisy is not such a bad thing. Hypocrisy can be a good thing in our society if it means advancing a sense of civility.

After all, it is often hypocrisy that fuels manners and etiquette, those little rules of conduct that do not quite rise to the level of law. We usually do not hold a door for somebody, shake hands, say please, avoid cursing or chew with our mouths closed because we enjoy doing these things. We do these things because we have been socially conditioned to conduct ourselves in a civilized, orderly fashion. This often means placing other peoples' concerns or feelings above our own self-expression and honesty. A person we know may be terribly dressed or have a horrible singing voice or have a weight problem, but we will avoid voicing harsh criticism to prevent hurt feelings or embarrassment. Rudeness is not a virtue. Instead of saying "That is the ugliest outfit I have ever seen," we may offer words of reassurance or encouragement or politely suggest changes.

Therein lies the hypocrisy. We feign something we really do not mean or feel. We are being hypocrites but only to the extent of being polite. In a society based on self-expression, the virtue of honesty can sometimes be carried too far. What purpose would be served by telling people what we honestly thought of them at every opportunity? We bite our tongues out of common decency. Call it controlled hypocrisy; call it politeness.

Manners are not legally compelled, but in many ways serve the purpose of laws. They allow us to get along with one another, even at the expense of curtailing our expression of feelings. The strange thing about manners is that nobody can make us be polite and often there might be no good reason to be polite but nonetheless we find our society functions much better when people are polite.

Judith Martin, Miss Manners, calls our deference to etiquette "the oldest social virtue, and an indispensable partner of morality."[21] In socializing our children, we teach them manners before we teach them broad moral concepts. We teach infants to share their toys with their play partners, not to hit others, not to shout or scream, to say thank you, and a myriad other small disciplines.

Manners are the shadows cast by virtues. They reflect our character. But in our changing culture, we have gotten it all backward. Acts of rudeness, disrespect or indecency are becoming more and more commonplace while random acts of politeness and etiquette are making the headlines in our newspapers. The day after the governor's election in 1994, I was driving home with my family down U.S. Route 1 in Miami. As I was driving, I noticed on the side of the road a small crowd that included Governor Lawton Chiles waving THANK YOU signs. In his thirty-five years in public office, Lawton Chiles has made it a tradition to travel the state the day after an election and thank people publicly for supporting his candidacy. When I recognized the governor, I pulled my car over, got out and went over to shake hands with him. It was the right thing to do; it was the polite thing to do. Just as we teach our children to be good sports and to shake the hands of the opposing team, my parents taught me that you should do these little things. I would expect anybody else to do the same. In fact, the truth of the matter is that I really did not even think about it. It was more of a conditioned reaction.

To my surprise, this small act of politeness made the news. Not just the local news, but the national news, thirty seconds on each major network. It was written about in *The Washington Post* and *The New York Times*. I am not kidding you and I am not bragging about this. I am just lamenting the fact that we have lost our sense of common decency. Thirty years ago, snubbing Lawton Chiles would have been considered newsworthy. Today, a small act of character or politeness makes the news.

The discipline problems we now face in our schools and with juvenile crime can often be traced directly to a failure by the parents to instill a sense of civility in their children. But it has become harder for parents to instill manners and common decency in their children when the world around them grows less polite, less respectful of others. Walk through the downtown of any of Florida's big cities during rush hour and you will experience motorists honking at one another; an obscene gesture flying from a commuter; a car stereo blaring so loudly that people in the adjacent cars cannot hear their own radios; a police officer directing traffic with a scowl, clearly perturbed about his role in this scene; people on car phones not paying attention to pedestrians in the crosswalk; a panhandler wading through traffic cursing at motorists who will not give him money. One car barely bumps the fender of another. Bang! Another lawsuit that will take three years to settle. One car cuts another off in an attempt to get to a parking space that in reality will save only a few yards' walk. Imagine all of this rudeness, all of this breakdown of civility at one busy street corner at 5:00 P.M. and that is only a microcosm of our society, with all its anger, indecency and impoliteness.

If we are looking for civility today, we think one of our best finds would be a silent hero from the game of baseball. We are talking about Cal Ripken, Jr., the Baltimore Oriole shortstop who surpassed Lou Gehrig's record of consecutive games played. Anybody watching baseball on the night Ripken broke that record could not help being touched by the emotion and pride of the moment. It was a special moment because Ripken has always been the epitome of a gentleman—well mannered, humble, quiet, hard-working. The record could not have gone to a better person. One has to question if the same outpouring of emotion would have occurred had the record been broken by some brash, ill-mannered, glitzed-up ballplayer who did not exemplify the elements of good sportsmanship. There is a lesson to be learned in Cal Ripken, Jr.

Even at the risk of being a little hypocritical it might be worth it to give honesty and freedom of self-expression a ding in order to preserve a society that for our children's sake should function under some common rules of decency and respect. White House speechwriter Peggy Noonan touched on this when she wrote about our "coarsened country" in her book *Life, Liberty and the Pursuit of Happiness.* She observed that "old America was full of grownups who were wonderful old hypocrites…. They were lying, but they were also, through their public action and words, making proper bows to an agreed upon ideal. They maintained a front, a façade. It was the price they all paid, perhaps without even thinking about it, to keep society going."[22] Today, we should all wonder whether our culture is better off in a world that no longer gives a nod to common decency, a world that is growing short on shortstops.

In the next three chapters we take you through the many cultural indicators. The first of these three looks at society's ills, the most tangible symptoms of our societal decline. These are problems that range from juvenile and violent crime to the waning of personal responsibility as seen by our proliferation of lawsuits and bankruptcies. Through the years, these problems have only gotten worse. The second of these three chapters lays out the cultural indicators relating to family and community. These little platoons have also decomposed through the years, leaving us with little ammunition to combat our social ills. Finally, we look at the cultural indicators relating to government. We shall see that while society's ills are getting worse, and families and communities fail in their functions, government thrives. We have created an artificial atmosphere where this creature called government grows bigger and bigger, draining us of our familial and communal spirit and responsibilities.

# CHAPTER THREE

# *Fourteen Days in May*

I T WAS TWO weeks in the life of Florida. Two weeks no different from any other two-week period in our lives. Neither police nor community leaders nor politicians nor researchers directed us to this particular two-week period. Rather, it was two weeks from the spring of 1995, randomly selected to take the temperature of our cultural climate in Florida. It would have made Hollywood proud! Through the fourteen-day period, the sights and sounds of a culture drifting through a sea of violence, dysfunction and oddity were captured. The visions and noises were familiar. Sights and sounds to which we have grown accustomed. What was once discordant has become harmonic, a dangerous melody.

Join us on this journey through our state.

Our fourteen days in May actually have a prelude, a couple of days earlier on Saturday, April 29, in St. Petersburg, Florida, with a family, a community and the sound of music. The music we hear is a hymn sung by a congregation and choir at the St. Mark Missionary Baptist Church. The tune is beautiful, "Home at Last, Ever to Rejoice." It is a young girl's eighteenth birthday. She is dressed in a silk and satin pink prom gown and wearing a white tiara adorned with rhinestones. There are flowers everywhere bursting with all the colors of the rainbow. About a thousand people have turned out for the young girl's birthday, but she is not with them. Kimberly Leshore is not attending her own birthday party. Rather, she is being buried. Kimberly was a junior and ROTC staff sergeant from Lakewood High School. She had plans to go into the air force and then to college. But almost a week earlier, a man approached the drive-through window of a Church's Chicken restaurant and told Kimberly to "give it up," shooting her before she had a chance to respond. The robber took no money. "It wasn't sickness. The man was a cold-blooded murderer. That's what he was," said the Reverend Theopolis Leshore, Kimberly's father.[1]

*Tuesday, May 2, 1995.* The body of a nude and beaten ten-year-old boy is found floating in the family swimming pool in West Palm Beach. The young boy, Andrew Schwarz, is the latest victim of child abuse and homicide, killed by his stepmother, Jessica Schwarz. Months later witnesses at her trial would testify how she constantly abused her stepson. According to their testimony, testimony that would result in a seventy-year sentence, Jessica Schwarz would humiliate Andrew by making him eat his meals next to the cat litter box and by making him run naked down neighborhood streets.

*Wednesday, May 3, 1995.* It is another typical day on Miami's Palmetto Expressway. Cars speeding out of control like high-speed grenades waiting for somebody to pull the pin. On May 3, the pin is pulled. Two cars— a Hyundai and a Jeep Cherokee—are traveling southbound on the expressway, swerving in and out of traffic and cutting each other off. Finally, both cars stop in an emergency lane after bumping each other. The driver of the Hyundai, a nineteen-year-old man, gets out and approaches an older man sitting in the Cherokee. The man sitting in the Cherokee, a former Miami police officer, has a semiautomatic weapon resting in his lap. The two men struggle with each other. The nineteen-year-old wrests the gun free, steps back from the Cherokee and, instead of walking away, methodically shoots and kills the man sitting in the Cherokee.

On that same day in Largo, Florida, our civil justice system was busy at work. Like any other courtroom scene, there was a judge, a court reporter, a lawyer and a witness. The particular witness in the box at the time was Charles Norwood. He was answering questions posed by Jerry Shannon, who, acting as his own attorney, had brought suit alleging that Charles Norwood stole his couch. Only this trial was different. Seven years earlier, Jerry Shannon, Florida prisoner number 11641, had murdered his wife. But Jerry Shannon's wife was also Charles Norwood's little sister. This day, Shannon was prosecuting his case against his ex–brother-in-law for removing from the house after the killing the belongings of the woman Shannon murdered. In the original suit, Shannon even included a claim against Charles Norwood for taking the gray silk dress Norwood's sister was to be buried in. The lawsuit that day was dismissed after Shannon rested his case. Defending against Shannon's claim cost Norwood and his insurance company thousands of dollars, and a family was forced to relive an awful murder. A teary-eyed Charles Norwood was left on that May day at the courthouse wondering how a remorseless killer could be so concerned about a couch.

"There was no remorse," says a New Port Richey sheriff's detective that same May day after arresting two teenagers, tenth- and eleventh-grade students at Gulf High School, for the murder of a seventy-one-year-old woman. The woman perished after a four-hour ordeal that included her rape and a drive to a grassy field a little south of her home where she was shot twice with her late husband's service revolver. It was alleged that the kids took thirty dollars and used the money to play video games at an arcade the next day. What was even more astonishing was that one of the teenagers helped police search for the body and appeared on the local TV news after the murders to say how much people would miss the elderly resident of a community known as Veterans Village.

*Thursday, May 4, 1995.* Let's continue our journey into north Florida. If you follow the coastline up the Gulf from New Port Richey, you will reach the town of Perry. There on this Thursday, a mildly retarded thirteen-year-old boy is sentenced to ten months in a juvenile facility. His crime: fatally shooting a prominent banker, church deacon and Air Force veteran from Monticello. However, the deceased had also conspired with the young boy's mother to obtain sex—from the boy. For eight months, the boy's mother was paid money in exchange for allowing the man to have sex with her mentally handicapped child.

On the same day, a Volusia County public schoolteacher was arrested for sexual battery for coaxing a six-teen-year-old boy into having sex with her in order to "save the world." Back in Largo, police discovered the dead bodies of three people in a mobile home—a husband, a wife and the wife's father, all killed in an apparent murder/suicide.

*Friday, May 5, 1995.* One month earlier, a family was destroyed in the northeast Florida town of Palatka, county seat for Putnam County. In that county's worst homicide case in its history, a mother, her three young daughters of two, four and seven years and their grandmother were found shot to death in their secluded home. A fifth victim, the husband, was found wounded at the crime scene. However, on this Friday, the husband of the murdered mother, the father of these three little girls and son-in-law to the grandmother, is indicted on five counts of first degree murder.

The same day in Clearwater, law enforcement officials discovered one of the worst cases of elder abuse in the state's history. Paramedics found, in her son's apartment, seventy-one-year-old Eleanor Templar on a couch surrounded by garbage and used diapers. Her body was so emaciated that hospital officials said she was the "living dead." She had been on the couch lying in feces and urine with worms, ants and roaches for six months straight. Her flesh was rotting away in places. When detectives questioned her son, Lewis Gene Templar, after his arrest, they described his demeanor as "oblivious" to the fact his mother had been abused.

*Saturday, May 6, 1995.* "Out here, we don't lock our doors half the time; we leave our keys in our cars. You live without thinking about violence. Our little sanctuary out here got violated," said columnist Hal Halcomb of

Treasure Island, a peaceful coastal community not too far from St. Petersburg. The violation Halcomb speaks of is the senseless, bizarre murder of a popular thirty-six-year-old restaurant cook. Shortly after midnight on Saturday, Charles Edward Hall and his wife stepped out of their bay-front duplex to tell five noisy teenagers who had gathered outside to quiet down. One of the teens, Michael Morin, whipped out a 20-gauge shotgun and killed Hall as Hall's wife stood by helplessly. A co-worker at the restaurant where Hall worked said in the aftermath, "Somebody stole something from me, stole a friend of mine."[2]

*Sunday, May 7, 1995.* Police in Sarasota arrest a former dentist for paying a hit man to kill his wife, who was found dead in February. The man is caught when he tries to hire an undercover cop to kill the first hit man.

*Monday, May 8, 1995.* Our second week again finds us in South Florida in the posh shopping district of Ft. Lauderdale somewhere on East Las Olas Boulevard. At 2:30 P.M., a Broward County transit bus screeches to a halt. Seven passengers and the driver run out of the bus screaming hysterically. Shopkeepers come running out of their stores to see what is happening. In this scene of confusion, people notice that there is a woman sitting on the stairs of the bus, rocking her two-year-old boy and screaming "Somebody help me!" Blood has begun to drip out of the back bus door while inside the bus one man is slumped forward in his seat and another is lying facedown in the aisle. Shortly before 2:30 in the afternoon, William Darren Harrison decided to commit suicide, but not before deciding, for no apparent reason, to shoot the passenger seated in front of him in the back of the head with a sawed-off shotgun. Harrison did not know the man he killed. Tragically, neither will the man's own two-year-old son.

*Tuesday, May 9, 1995.* A ninth-grade girl becomes the twenty-first sexual battery victim in an Alachua County school in 1994/1995. Her assailant is a fellow ninth-grade student at Gainesville High School. This attack marks six more sexual assaults than last year's number of fifteen in the Alachua County schools.

*Wednesday, May 10, 1995.* We finally hear some good news, relatively speaking. In Tampa, an appellate court upholds the attempted murder convictions of Mark Kohut and Charles Rourk, ending their appeals in the state court system. You might remember these two men. They were the ones who on New Year's Day in 1993 abducted visiting New York stock brokerage clerk Christopher Wilson in a Tampa suburb. Then they drove Wilson, an African American, to a deserted field, doused him with gasoline, called him "Nigger" and set him on fire.

*Thursday, May 11, 1995.* Thursday provides us with a less violent but equally disturbing story about our culture. In 1991, a woman was nearly involved in a car accident in Palm Harbor, just north of Clearwater. In trying to avoid a crash that had occurred ahead of her, this woman's car spun out of control hitting nothing. There was no damage to her car and the woman was not injured. In 1993, after finding out that Nationwide Insurance Company insured the man who caused the accident, the woman made repeated demands through her own efforts and that of a lawyer against the insurance company for $25,000 in damages. The woman claimed that the "almost-accident" triggered damaging memories of childhood sexual abuse. She represented to the insurance investigator that she had had no recollections of this childhood abuse until the car incident. However, in 1990, the woman had told a Tampa women's magazine that she was dealing with the consequence of childhood sexual abuse. She had also told police that she realized the abuse in 1988. On Thursday, May 11, the woman is arrested for insurance fraud.

*Friday, May 12, 1995.* Ft. Pierce. A mother of a twelve-year-old girl is arrested for prostituting her daughter in exchange for twenty dollars' worth of crack cocaine. The mother, oblivious to the atrocity she has just caused, sits outside the bedroom and smokes the crack while her daughter is inside being raped by a twenty-two-year-old man.

We close our two weeks with the sounds of music again. There is singing. It comes from a little farther south in Homestead, Florida. Outside a home, members of the Faith Deliverance Church have gathered in a circle and are holding hands and singing. They are the friends and family of the church's pastor, Mary Ann Lee Hughes, and they have come to pray. The forty-six-year-old pastor was found by her husband today in the closet of their home. She had been murdered. Her twenty-three-year-old daughter described the scene, "Somebody shot her, shot her and shot her."[3]

Our two weeks are over. Look into the faces of the people in Florida and what do we see? The faces that breathe life into the numbers and trends of the last twenty to thirty years. The numerical indicators that follow in these chapters serve only to show us the depth of the social problems described in our journey across the state. Take some time to read through the chapters as we present Florida's cultural indicators—the statistics and trends that bear out our cultural erosion. You will see that many facets of Florida's society have been touched by violent crime, juvenile delinquency, waning education, increased child poverty, young adult suicide and a clogged legal system. In many cases, you will see that Florida's cultural decline is occurring at a rate faster than the rest of our nation, showing now more than ever the need for character and virtue in our society.

The cultural indicators show us the victims of Florida multiplied by hundreds and thousands. The numbers are more impersonal than the human beings you just encountered, but try to see each number as we do—as a Kimberly Leshore or a Mary Ann Lee Hughes.

# Crime in Florida

The most prominent feature of our cultural landscape today is the breakdown of order as manifested by our crime problem. Next to Disney World, the crime problem is probably what comes into the minds of most people when they think of the Sunshine State. Crime is the ultimate indicator because of its immediate impact on a family or community. The crack of a gun can leave a whole family or community scarred for generations. Unlike our problems with poverty or education, crime is instantaneous and indiscriminate of race, age and background.

Over the last thirty years, the effects of violent crime have trickled down to our youngest age groups. It is most disturbing when children are both the perpetrators and the victims. Children are more likely to commit crime and more likely to perish from it. Never before have so many parents had to bury so many sons and daughters. In 1960, homicides were not a serious problem among our children, especially children ages one to four. One would think with kids that age that homicide would never be a problem. After all, we are talking about the murder of infants and babies. In 1960, the leading causes of death among children ages one to four in Florida included influenza, meningitis, cancer and accidents. Homicide was way down the list. In that same year, there were only nine homicides statewide for children in the age group of five through fourteen.

Thirty years later, murder is the third leading cause of death among Florida's infants and toddlers. In 1994, there were thirty-three children murdered between the ages of one and four. Between the ages of five and fourteen, the number of murders is four times what the number was in 1960.

But this is only one small aspect of our expanding crime problem over the last thirty years. Our state is first in the nation in both total crime rates and violent crime rates, making Florida the "Crime Capital of America."[4] Between 1960 and 1994, Florida's crime rate per 100,000 persons increased by 203 percent, a rate faster than that experienced by the rest of the nation.

As for the growth in total crimes committed, Florida blew the rest of the nation away. Between 1960 and 1994, the number of total crimes committed in Florida increased by an incredible 744 percent, compared to the national rate increase of 318 percent. In 1993, approximately one of every fourteen crimes in America was committed in the State of Florida.

Florida's crime problem is magnified in our cities, which lead the nation in crime rates. For example, the Federal Bureau of Investigation released its national crime figures for 1994 among cities of 100,000 persons or more. The top three cities in the nation with the most crime, starting with the worst, were Ft. Lauderdale, Tampa and Miami. And if those in north Florida thought crime was only something to be experienced by the big cities to the south, think again. The state capital, Tallahassee, had the eleventh highest crime rate among major cities in the nation—worse than Orlando, St. Petersburg and Jacksonville.

Crime touches all of us in Florida, but no crime frightens us more than violent crime: murder, rape, robbery, aggravated assault. In Florida, violent crime has spiraled out of control over the last three decades. In 1960, the violent crime rate per 100,000 people in

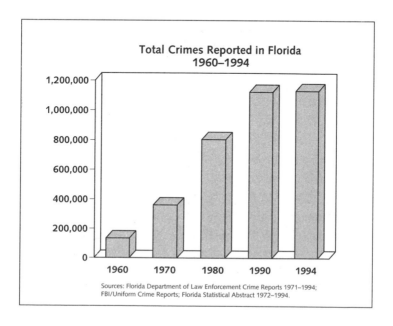

Total Crimes Reported in Florida
1960–1994

Sources: Florida Department of Law Enforcement Crime Reports 1971–1994;
FBI/Uniform Crime Reports; Florida Statistical Abstract 1972–1994.

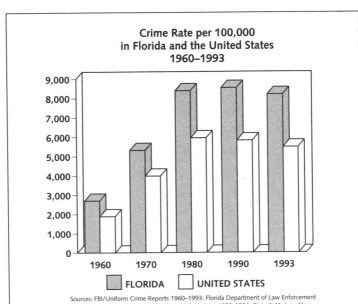

## Crime Rate per 100,000 in Florida and the United States 1960–1993

FLORIDA    UNITED STATES

Sources: FBI/Uniform Crime Reports 1960–1993; Florida Department of Law Enforcement Crime Reports 1971–1993; Florida Statistical Abstract 1972–1991; State & Metropolitan Data Book; Statistical Abstract of the United States 1992.

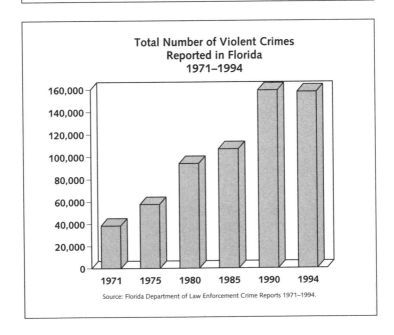

## Total Number of Violent Crimes Reported in Florida 1971–1994

Source: Florida Department of Law Enforcement Crime Reports 1971–1994.

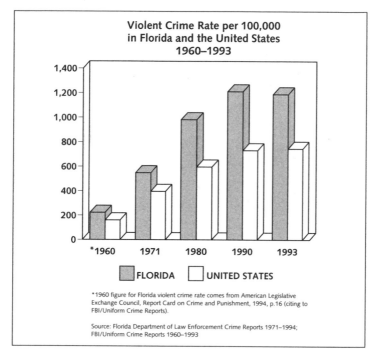

Violent Crime Rate per 100,000
in Florida and the United States
1960–1993

*1960 figure for Florida violent crime rate comes from American Legislative Exchange Council, Report Card on Crime and Punishment, 1994, p.16 (citing to FBI/Uniform Crime Reports).

Source: Florida Department of Law Enforcement Crime Reports 1971–1994; FBI/Uniform Crime Reports 1960–1993

Florida was 223. In 1994, the violent crime rate was 1154, an astonishing 417 percent increase. During that same period, Florida's population increased by only 182 percent.

What is worse than these numbers is the growing feeling that there is nowhere we can be safe from violent crime. Consider the recent shooting of a Little League baseball coach during a game in Tampa or the accidental shooting of two persons in a Clearwater park at July Fourth festivities. Incidents like these dampen our spirit and cause the breakdown of trust among Floridians and the government created to protect them. Wherever we go, we are always on guard. Potential crime now affects our lifestyle every day. The absurdity of it all can be found in a recent edition of an airline in-flight shopping catalog. On a page titled "The Safety Zone," readers are enticed to purchase the "Safe-T-Man: Your Personal Bodyguard." For those who have not seen the Safe-T-Man around, he is a simulated 180-pound six-foot-tall latex man with airbrushed facial growth. The advertisement, obviously directed at women, states that Safe-T-Man is there "to give others the impression that you have the protection of a male guardian with you while at home alone or driving in your car." The catalog goes on to show Safe-T-Man sitting in a living-room chair, Safe-T-Man riding shotgun with his female companion and Safe-T-Man being stuffed into a suitcase. The advertisement is so ridiculous that it makes you want to double over in laughter. But this is serious. People now really feel like they have to rely on Safe-T-Man. That part should make us want to cry.

The routineness of our encounters with crime in Florida can be put into perspective succinctly. Every day in Florida there are 3 murders, 20 rapes, 124 robberies and 336 auto thefts. Put another way, there is 1 murder every 7 hours and 30 minutes. One reported rape every 1 hour and 12 minutes. One reported robbery every 12 minutes. One reported auto theft every 4 minutes and 18 seconds. In South Florida, auto thefts are so high that collectively the three counties of Palm Beach, Broward and Dade would rank ninth among all the states in the nation.[5] And despite some recent decreases in the violent crime rate, there is still 1 violent crime committed every 3 minutes and 19 seconds in Florida. The number of violent crimes has increased 3 times over since 1971, and that only counts for the *reported* violent crimes. So these numbers might be even higher considering that many crimes never get reported.

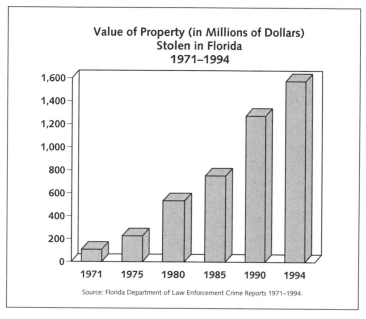

**Value of Property (in Millions of Dollars) Stolen in Florida 1971–1994**

Source: Florida Department of Law Enforcement Crime Reports 1971–1994.

Finally, our growing crime problem has an economic impact on our lives. Crime is the most severe tax on a community that has ever been created. The value of property stolen in Florida is an example of this. In 1971, $107 million in property was taken in thefts and burglaries, and by 1994, that dollar amount had increased almost fifteenfold, to $1.5 billion in stolen property. This crime tax goes way beyond the value of stolen property. High crime rates rob communities of potential economic growth as businesses look elsewhere to set up shop. Insurance premiums in Florida are sky high because of our bulging crime rate. Because of the great volume of auto thefts in Florida, an average automobile insurance premium is $739.81, with that number much higher in the cities.[6] So not only are we paying more in actual taxes to combat the crime problem, but we are also spending more on private security officers, home security systems and antitheft devices with names like The Club and Safe-T-Man.

# Juvenile Crime in Florida

Virgil wrote in *The Aeneid* that from a single crime, know the nation.[7] From a single crime, know our state. In Tallahassee at the Cobb Middle School in June 1994, an art teacher requested as she passed out final exams that one of her students sit down. The student, a fourteen-year-old, exploded and repeatedly punched the teacher in the face, giving her black eyes, a chipped tooth, a cut lip and other bruises. The teacher was covered in blood from head to toe. The fourteen-year-old boy had to be pulled off her. Ask the art teacher what was most shocking about this attack and she will tell you plainly that it was not that a student had attacked a teacher. Teacher assaults are up in Florida. She will tell you that it was not the vision of a young boy striking an older woman. What was most shocking to her was that during the attack another student was looking on chanting "Hit her, hit her. Kill her, kill her." A 1995 survey by the United Teachers of Dade County found that almost 10 percent of the teachers responding had been assaulted by a student during the last school year.[8]

Where did all this youthful rage come from? Some say you can see it in their eyes—cold, lifeless eyes that do not understand the sanctity of life, compassion or the difference between right and wrong.

In March 1995, the Florida Department of Law Enforcement released its annual crime report for 1994, which showed minimal increases and decreases in a

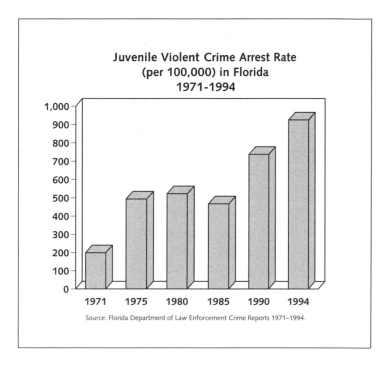

**Juvenile Violent Crime Arrest Rate (per 100,000) in Florida 1971-1994**

Source: Florida Department of Law Enforcement Crime Reports 1971–1994.

variety of crime figures. Yet next to these marginal changes, we found that the number of juveniles arrested increased by more than 27 percent statewide in just one year.[9] A juvenile was arrested for murder every other day last year in Florida. According to the U.S. Department of Justice, Florida's juvenile violent crime arrest rate ranks second in the nation, behind New York. Since 1971, when the Florida Department of Law Enforcement first began segregating juvenile arrests, the juvenile violent crime arrest rate has increased almost 365 percent.

Not only is there more crime committed by juveniles, but it is also escalating a whole lot earlier. Arguments that at one time would result in a fistfight on the school playground now become shoot-outs. It is disheartening

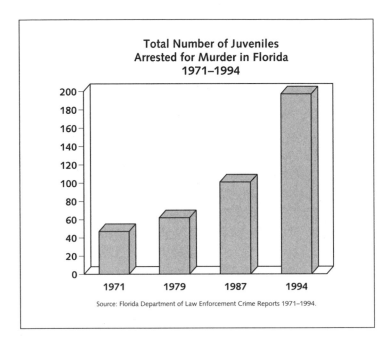

**Total Number of Juveniles
Arrested for Murder in Florida
1971–1994**

Source: Florida Department of Law Enforcement Crime Reports 1971–1994.

to constantly read about children, some under age ten, shooting at each other.

Since 1971, the total number of juveniles arrested has increased by 51 percent from 74,243 to 111,739. At the same time, the number of juveniles arrested for murder has increased by 319 percent. For those who are thinking that we are being disingenuous because Florida is a fast growing state, take note. Since 1971, Florida's juvenile population growth has been approximately 25 percent. Clearly, we have got a problem, and it's only getting worse. According to a recent report by the U.S. Department of Justice, the number of juveniles arrested will double by the year 2010. Florida's number will more than double as our teen population is expected to increase more than the national average.[10]

It is worth noting that juvenile crime is not limited

by gender. It has been reported that juvenile violent felony arrests in Florida are rising faster among young girls than they are among young boys. A vivid example of this gender twist is the killing of a Palm Beach County cabdriver by three young girls over a six-dollar cab fare. The girl who allegedly pulled the trigger was seventeen years old. The other girls involved were only fifteen years old and thirteen years old. Stephanie Powell, the thirteen-year-old sixth grader, confessed to the murder in the courtroom as she literally sucked her thumb. The Florida Department of Juvenile Justice reported that for a five-year period ending on July 1, 1994, the number of felony arrests among Florida girls went up 83 percent while the number of felony arrests among boys increased by 27 percent.[11]

# Education in Florida

The Florida Department of Corrections recently reported that of all the inmates in Florida's prisons only 8.6 percent have any type of education beyond the twelfth grade. Forty-four percent of the 3.8 million mothers enrolled nationwide in AFDC lack high school diplomas. Crime and welfare and education. Who can doubt that education does not influence our crime and poverty levels? While it might be difficult to prove that the lack of education causes crime or poverty or other social scourges, the numbers suggest that if a person possesses an adequate education, he or she is less likely to end up in prison or on the welfare rolls.

Our character deficit in Florida is not only reflected by the levels of crime and poverty but by poor academic performance as well. In the last three decades, public schools have moved away from teaching character and have become arenas for some of our children's least virtuous activities, such as gang violence, teenage sex, drug abuse and alcoholism. Today, our public school systems are forced to install metal detectors at their front doors and to hire private security officers, but school boards continue to debate the appropriateness of teaching virtue and character in the schools!

At the University of Texas, all publications have on their title pages a quote attributed to Sam Houston. It reads, "The benefits of education and of useful knowledge, generally diffused through a community, are essential to preservation of free government." This statement recognizes that we cannot become a self-governing society unless we possess the education and knowledge necessary for this task. To this end, education is the great equalizer in society. It is the one thing that unequivocally closes the gap between the haves and have-nots and it is available to all. Abraham Lincoln is the classic example of a poor backwoodsman who through a voracious appetite for reading as a child came to walk the path of knowledge to greatness. Today, a young person need not sit at home and teach herself how to read as Lincoln did. A young person who attends school, is serious about learning and works hard to attend college can realize her dreams through public education. Yet more than 50 percent of our children in public schools read below basic reading levels. In this generation, our educational institutions have to both teach and constantly struggle against the effects of drugs, gangs, teen pregnancy and other distractions that pull our young citizens away from the fountain of knowledge.

Unfortunately, even if a child attends school every day and tries to drink from the fountain, Florida does not guarantee that child an adequate education. To illustrate, consider the Readiness for College test program that began just five years ago in Florida. In 1990, the state began testing the college readiness of students who graduated from the Florida public school system and chose to attend college at a Florida public college or university. The Readiness for College tests were to determine on an annual basis how many students graduating from Florida public schools needed remedial level course work to bring them up to college level reading, math and writing.

In the first year of the test, 1990–1991, 63 percent of the students participating in the test were determined by the state to be prepared for college and needed no remedial education. Conversely, in the first year of the test, a staggering 37 percent of college-bound Florida public high school graduates were not prepared for college and needed some kind of remedial course work to enable them to perform at the college level.

The news gets worse. For the last three academic years, the number of Florida public high school graduates ready for college has actually declined. The most recent published test scores for the academic year 1993–1994 show that more than 42 percent of college-bound Florida public high school graduates are not prepared for college. Of Florida's sixty-seven counties, a total of eighteen had 50 percent or less of their college-bound high school graduates prepared for college course work!

Florida has also recently participated in another series of performance-based tests known as the

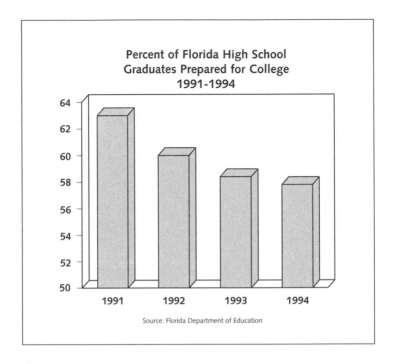

Percent of Florida High School
Graduates Prepared for College
1991-1994

Source: Florida Department of Education

National Assessment of Educational Progress (NAEP) tests. These tests focus on our elementary and junior high school students' proficiency levels in math and reading. In 1992, Florida eighth and fourth graders took the NAEP mathematics test. Only 18 percent of Florida eighth graders taking the test were at or above proficient in eighth-grade-level math and only 2 percent were advanced while 45 percent were determined to be below a basic level in mathematics![12] The fourth graders did not fair much better: Only 14 percent of them were at or above proficient.

The Florida fourth graders took part in the NAEP reading test in 1992 and 1994. Sadly, the 1994 scores actually declined slightly from the 1992 scores, ranking Florida's fourth graders thirty-sixth out of thirty-nine

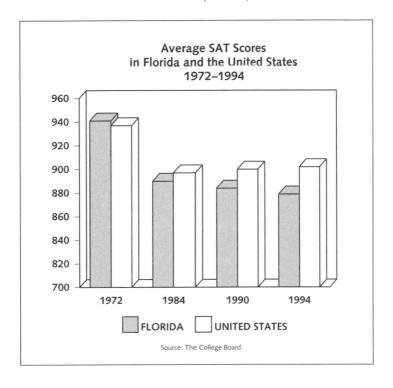

Average SAT Scores
in Florida and the United States
1972–1994

FLORIDA    UNITED STATES

Source: The College Board.

states participating in the nation. Once again, only 19 percent of Florida's fourth graders were reading at or above proficient while 53 percent of them had below basic reading skills.[13]

Finally, the last and most often cited indicator reflecting student performance in Florida is the SAT. Of the indicators mentioned previously, the SAT is the only consistent indicator of academic performance in Florida tracked over a number of years. Unfortunately, but consistent with our other findings, the average SAT score in Florida has dropped dramatically since the College Board first kept records of Florida scores in 1972. In that year, the average SAT score in Florida was 941, and the national average was 937. However, by

1994, the average SAT score in Florida had dropped 62 points while the national average had declined by only 35 points. Florida now ranks forty-fifth in the nation in average SAT scores. But fear not! SAT test scores in Florida should increase soon. Not because students are getting any smarter but because the College Board has decided to boost scores by inflating the average. It has been called recentering. Although it should not change a student's standing among fellow test takers, it will have the effect of making every student's performance appear better.

But even if we go beyond test taking, we can still see that our educational system is failing our children. Take graduation rates in the State of Florida. According to the U.S. Department of Education, Florida ranked forty-seventh nationwide with a 62 percent graduation rate. The ranking was just barely enough to propel us ahead of Louisiana, South Carolina and Texas. Florida's graduation rate for the academic year 1993–1994 was still almost ten percentage points below the national average and was down slightly from Florida's 1980 graduation rate. However, as we will see in Chapter Five, public spending on education in Florida has been increasing at rates that make any decline in the graduation rates and test scores an embarrassment.

Based on these indicators, here is a look at Florida's future. Our public schools are generating the following results in a downward trend: A little more than one third of our young people will continue to graduate from high school with the core competencies that will allow them to pursue higher education and the fountain of knowledge. These people will by and large be the achievers who will carry the heavier burden in shaping our state. In a knowledge-based society, in an increasingly global economy, this third will live comfortably. On the other hand, one third of Florida's young people will not graduate from high school at all. Their horizons will be shorter; their dreams will be narrower. They will have a difficult time keeping up with rapid global and societal changes. Often, they will create demands on our society rather than produce for society. The remaining one third of our young people will be somewhere in the middle. They will graduate from high school but in order to continue drinking from the fountain of knowledge, they will need remedial help. Only a little better off than those who do not graduate at all, these young people will still be woefully unprepared to compete in today's sophisticated economic and social structure. At a time when their diplomas need to mean more, they will mean less.

# Poverty in Florida

It was 1964 when President Lyndon B. Johnson stood before a joint session of Congress and declared an "unconditional war on poverty." Yet since the war on poverty began, the gap between the haves and the havenots in Florida has only increased. While personal income is growing in Florida, so too is the percentage of persons receiving public assistance. All told, the percent of Florida's population receiving AFDC benefits and food stamps has increased over the last thirty years. Aid to Families with Dependent Children began as a way of providing some means of support to widows under the Social Security Act of 1935. Today, however,

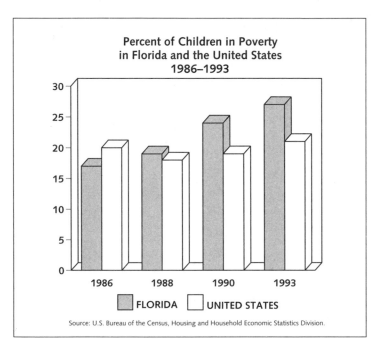

**Percent of Children in Poverty
in Florida and the United States
1986–1993**

FLORIDA    UNITED STATES

Source: U.S. Bureau of the Census, Housing and Household Economic Statistics Division.

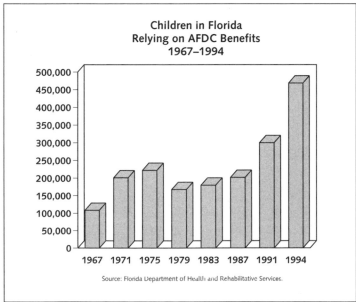

**Children in Florida
Relying on AFDC Benefits
1967–1994**

Source: Florida Department of Health and Rehabilitative Services.

AFDC goes mainly to mothers who give birth out of wedlock. In 1960, 1.7 percent of Florida's population relied on AFDC benefits. In 1994, almost 5 percent of Florida's population relied on AFDC. Similarly, in 1971, the first full year of the statewide food stamp program, roughly 6 percent of Florida's population received food stamps. Now, almost 11 percent of all Floridians receive food stamps. This means that the public costs of poverty are growing. Today, nearly $1.1 billion is spent in the State of Florida on AFDC and $1.3 billion is spent on food stamps, with no sign that we are advancing in the war against poverty.

The poverty explosion in Florida has inevitably affected our children. In fact, children in the United States have been found to be poorer than those in almost all other Western industrialized nations.[14] In Florida, our children are in even worse shape. Since 1986, the percent of children in poverty across the nation has remained steady at about 21 percent. During this same period, the percent of children in poverty in Florida has increased to a twelve-year high of 26.9 percent of all children in Florida. Since 1981, the total number of children in poverty in the State of Florida has increased by 56 percent. According to the latest figures, Florida is ranked forty-sixth in the nation in terms of the percent of children at or below the poverty level. This puts us ahead of only West Virginia, Mississippi, Louisiana and Tennessee. Furthermore, the number of children actually relying on AFDC benefits has increased dramatically. In 1994, the number of Florida children relying on AFDC was 333 percent greater than the number of children relying on AFDC in 1966.

# Child, Teen and Young Adult Suicide in Florida

It recently came to our attention that in Florida more people commit suicide each year than are murdered. To be exact, in 1994, 735 more people committed suicide than were murdered. It is also worth noting that a greater number of those persons committing suicide each year are teenagers and young adults. In fact, the fastest growing segment of the population dying by suicide is fifteen- to twenty-four-year-olds.

The teen and young adult suicide rate in Florida has seen two separate growth spurts. Between 1960 and 1980, the suicide rate for this group increased by 139 percent. Then between 1980 and 1985, the suicide rate actually fell. However, over the last ten years, Florida has once again seen the steady rise in the teen and young adult suicide rate. Between 1985 and 1994, the suicide rate has increased from 11.9 percent to 12.5 percent. In 1993, the teen and young adult suicide rate was 14.4 percent. A recent survey conducted by the publisher of *Who's Who Among American High School Students* reports that among the 3177 students across the country who were questioned, 46 percent knew someone their age who had tried to commit suicide.[15]

The disturbing part about this trend is that nobody seems to have a good reason for *why* the young adult suicide rate has been growing. One professor at the University of South Florida says that many suicides are based on hopelessness. "It's a feeling that the future has nothing to offer."[16] Perhaps as the rest of our culture moves in the wrong direction, young adults in Florida sense the despair in society. Other possible explana-

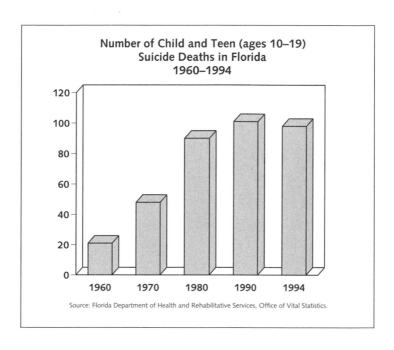

**Number of Child and Teen (ages 10–19) Suicide Deaths in Florida 1960–1994**

Source: Florida Department of Health and Rehabilitative Services, Office of Vital Statistics.

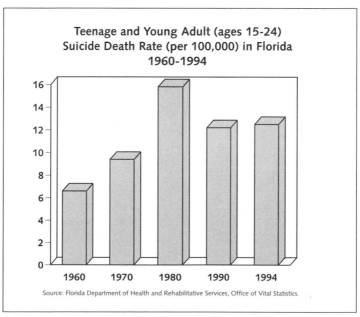

**Teenage and Young Adult (ages 15-24) Suicide Death Rate (per 100,000) in Florida 1960-1994**

Source: Florida Department of Health and Rehabilitative Services, Office of Vital Statistics.

tions for the high suicide rates implicate our cultural problems of today. Family problems with separation and divorce and the availability of drugs and alcohol are often cited as root causes of suicide. One thing is certain: The high teen and young adult suicide rate is as much a part of our cultural decline as crime, poverty or poor education.

At a recent funeral for a popular West Palm Beach teenager who committed suicide, a family friend, Helen Mays, spoke of the responsibility of the whole community for teenage suicides. "Is this death a rallying point for something?" she asked a packed church. "We have to talk to one another. We have to talk to one another's children ..."[17]

# Child and Elder Abuse in Florida

There can be no greater tragedy in the world than the beating death of a child. A few days after Christmas 1994, we here in South Florida were outraged by a story of child abuse in its worst manifestation. On Christmas Eve, an infant in Miami was shaken to death by his father, who was trying to feed his baby. The baby would not stop crying, so the father began shaking his infant son. He shook the baby so violently that it finally went limp in his hands and stopped breathing. The baby died after suffering severe brain damage. He was only three weeks old. The father had been released early from prison after serving part of a five-year sentence for abusing two other children from a previous relationship. Those children had suffered cracked skulls and ribs and broken legs as a result of their father's abuse.

A few months after this tragedy, a police officer and his wife in Rockledge, Florida, were charged with felony child abuse. It was believed that their four children, who were only two years old to four years old, had been kept starved prisoners of their parents in a dark room for years. The children were so starved that they had gnawed on wood in the room in an effort to quench their hunger.

Each year the number of sickening stories of abuse of our children in Florida increases. In 1994, more than one hundred children in our state were killed by adults who were supposed to be taking care of them. The dearth of character associated with this crime speaks for itself. No government, no program can curb whatever drives a parent to murder his or her own child. It is sick. And yet it goes on.

Florida is worse than most states when it comes to the percentage of children being abused. In 1993, the U.S. Census Bureau found that Florida ranked third in the nation among states in child abuse. In another study, conducted by the University of Missouri and the U.S. Centers for Disease Control and Prevention, researchers compared data from 1979 to 1988 and also ranked Florida third in the nation for child abuse rates, basing their analysis on death certificates and crime reports.[18]

The four worst cities in America for children dying as a result of abuse are, in order: Phoenix, Orlando, Tampa–St. Petersburg and Miami. In Orlando, the worst of the Florida cities, it was estimated that nine children are killed by child abuse each year. Researchers also confirmed that our cultural indicators do not operate in a vacuum. They found higher incidents of abuse and neglect where there were higher rates of poverty, broken homes, and drug or alcohol abuse.

In an effort to curb abuse of children, the Florida Department of Health and Rehabilitative Services has set up hot lines for persons to call to report instances of child abuse. However, this has not proven effective at stopping the problem and, in fact, has created a new problem: the unjustified reporting of parents who spank their children for disciplinary purposes. It's a classic example of government making a bad problem worse.

Equally as heinous as child abuse is the abuse or neglect of a senior citizen who cannot care for himself. Since Florida is home to so many retirees, elder abuse has fast become a serious problem. In May 1995, the National Center on Elder Abuse reported that over the last eight years, accounts of domestic elder abuse increased by 106 percent. In Florida, the number of elder abuse reports increased from 14,273 in 1988–1989 to 17,480 in 1992–1993.[19] Roughly 75 percent of the abuse of our elderly is occurring at the hands of a relative, compared to only 25 percent who were abused by a service provider or a stranger.

In Florida, our sixty-five-year-old and older population has increased by 160 percent since 1970. As this segment of our population continues to rise and more elders become dependent on their children, incidents of elder abuse in Florida will grow. More relatives will face the stress and frustration of caring for loved ones and, without proper self-control, will inevitably crack. Also, the scope of the problem may even be greater when we consider that the juveniles of this generation, those who are committing more crimes and acts of violence than ever before, will grow up to become the adults charged with the responsibility of caring for us. It will be an ironic twist of fate when we subject our own personal well-being to the juveniles whom we wish we taught to be more virtuous!

# Personal Responsibility in Florida

The SS *Norway* is a cruise ship that runs between Miami and the Caribbean, and like any cruise ship, the *Norway* offers entertainment, drink, gambling and other typical cruise ship activities. It also offers sumo wrestling. Yes, passengers on the *Norway* can wrestle each other sumo style in one of the ship's lounges. And that is just what one female passenger from New Jersey did on a recent cruise. Passengers who choose to test their bumping skills as well as their common sense are strapped into a big inflatable suit made to resemble the Stay-Puff Marshmallow man. Two passengers, now limited in mobility by all the inflation, are allowed to bump each other around for a bit on a wrestling mat. On this particular cruise, the passenger from New Jersey bumped with a friend of hers before an audience in the Checkers Lounge and she won. The passenger then entered a second match. This time, however, her inflated opponent lost her balance and gracelessly fell on the defending champ's right foot, resulting in a broken foot bone. The story does not end with the ignoble finish of our passenger's sumo wrestling career. Upon return to port, this passenger filed a lawsuit in Dade County's already bursting judicial system against the operator of the SS *Norway*, Kloster Cruise Limited. In filing this lawsuit, the passenger asserted that the operator of the ship should be held responsible for her injuries.

This case presents us with an interesting question that is coming up more and more often in Florida and in the nation as well. Who is responsible? Our society's response to that question has changed over time. Once, there were common principles and understood norms to guide the scenario above. It used to be that our normal gut response to such injury would have been one of acceptance and embarrassment. You offer to dress up as a Stay-Puff Marshmallow woman. You offer to wrestle. You hurt your foot. You are chagrined. How do you tell your friends? Stuff happens. End of story.

Today, however, the gut response is different. Now whenever we injure ourselves, we find others to point the finger at. We become "entitled" to compensation. We have rights. We say, "Okay, so I threw caution to the wind and dressed up as a human beach ball just to pummel my best friend. They should have made the darned suit fluffier!" It's not good enough to admit that we messed up or that there are some things that just cannot be controlled. At what point did we begin rewarding persons for their own bad judgment? At what point did we displace justice with entitlement?

Lawyer bashing has always been fashionable and is even more so now as the battle over tort reform continues in Washington, D.C. However, make no mistake about it, this is not primarily a lawyer problem. This is not a problem with our laws or even with our civil justice system. The legal profession is a service industry governed by the laws of supply and demand. Its job is to respond to the demand. The more people out there who are willing to file lawsuits, declare bankruptcy or submit workers' compensation claims, the more lawyers there will be to help serve as guides through the rocky shoals of justice. There will always be lawyers. But the lawsuit begins with the person who feels he is entitled to something from somebody, not with the lawyer. It is, once again, a matter of character.

Between 1978 and 1994, the total number of lawsuits filed in Florida's state court system increased by 78 percent. Between 1971 and 1993, the number of lawsuits filed in federal courts in Florida increased by 187 percent. Both numbers exceeded the rate of population growth during the same time frame. And in true supply and demand fashion, as the number of lawsuits has increased, so has the number of lawyers. The number of

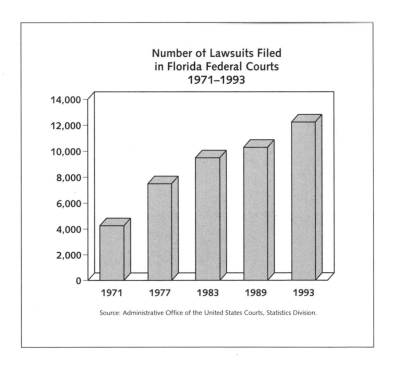

**Number of Lawsuits Filed
in Florida Federal Courts
1971–1993**

Source: Administrative Office of the United States Courts, Statistics Division.

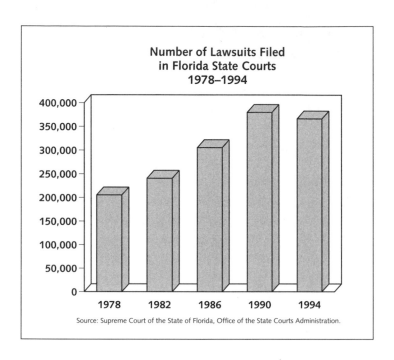

**Number of Lawsuits Filed in Florida State Courts 1978–1994**

Source: Supreme Court of the State of Florida, Office of the State Courts Administration.

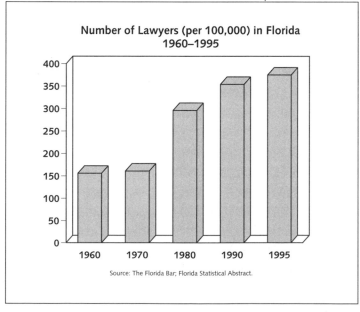

**Number of Lawyers (per 100,000) in Florida 1960–1995**

Source: The Florida Bar; Florida Statistical Abstract.

lawyers per 100,000 Floridians increased 140 percent between 1960 and 1995. These numbers suggest different things.

First, there has been a rise in legitimate lawsuits. Our character deficit has contributed to this as more and more people are willing to go back on their obligations or to infringe on other peoples' rights. More people now break contracts; more people are now willing to injure their fellowman. Second, there has been a rise in not-so-legitimate lawsuits, often referred to as frivolous lawsuits. This too is part of our character deficit. The increasing litigation reflects our willingness to redefine responsibility. More people feel entitled to compensation. It also shows the breakdown in our culture's informal mechanisms for settling disputes, mechanisms such as civility or business customs. Either way, the news is not good.

Studies seem to suggest that the litigation explosion is a result of both. Although the stories about personal injury cases and their lawyers always make good reading, the truth is, at least in federal courts, it is business disputes, mostly contract cases, that are jamming the judicial system. According to one study, the number of contract cases in federal courts increased by 232 percent between 1960 and 1988 while during the same time the number of tort cases increased by 128 percent.[20] This seems to reflect changing business customs and turning away from agreed-upon obligations.

Concurrently, personal injury and product liability cases still comprise the second largest block of cases backlogged in the federal court system. And, of course, the increase in tort cases reflects some of our changed feelings toward entitlement. For example, one study by the Insurance Research Council (IRC) reviewed automobile accident and injury claim patterns in every state from 1980 to 1993. The IRC found that today Americans are far more likely to claim auto injuries than in 1980, even though accident rates have actually declined since then. Nationwide, the injury liability claims rate has increased by 64 percent since 1980. According to the executive director of IRC, "What we see is more claimants with sprains and strains, more claimants hiring attorneys, and more nonemergency treatment of injuries with chiropractors and physical therapists. The data suggest people who previously would not have filed injury liability claims for minor injuries are now becoming claimants."[21] Contrary to popular belief, this kind of response hits the people harder than the insurance company. The willingness of more people to bring unnecessary claims to insurance companies costs the average Floridian hundreds of dollars a year in increased automobile insurance premiums.

Our legal system is also bulging as a result of an increasing amount of frivolous lawsuits brought by Florida State inmates. Prison lawsuits cost us, to the tune of $2 million each year. The Florida attorney general has to spend a significant portion of time defending against the eighty lawsuits filed each month by Florida prisoners. Such suits reflect the ultimate lunacy of criminal rights run awry. Consider some of the suits we have to subsidize. Inmate Robert Procup sued because he wanted his meals served on china instead of paper plates. Florida prisoner Robert Attwood sued when he found gristle on a turkey leg.[22] Since 1970, lawsuits like these have increased by 1550 percent nationally—further evidence that our society has allowed the "rights" movement to be taken to the extreme.

Another area of the law that reflects poorly on personal responsibility is the number of bankruptcies filed in Florida. Bankruptcy is a legal device that enables individuals and businesses to forgo their debts and begin anew. It is a recognition that a person or company has spent more money than it has or owes more money than it can pay. The bankruptcy then becomes the legal excuse for not being held responsible for the debts owed. Perhaps reflecting Florida's debtor-favorable bankruptcy exemptions, between 1960 and 1994, the total number of bankruptcies filed each year in Florida increased by an incredible 8586 percent! On a national basis, the total number of bankruptcies filed has increased only 656 percent, still a significant number but nowhere near the rate of Florida's increase.

Just as more Floridians appear willing to test the limits of insurance companies and creditors, so too are they willing to commit fraud to recover workers' compensation benefits. The statistics show that there are more cases of workers' compensation fraud in Florida now than ever before. Since 1991, when the Florida Department of Insurance first began keeping track, the number of workers' compensation fraud cases has increased by 47 percent. With about 25 percent of all compensation claims being false, Floridians spend an extra $400 million a year to absorb the increase in premiums directly attributed to fraud.[23]

Our waning personal responsibility can be tracked in a number of ways, but it seems that our ever increasing use of the legal system provides the best example. So allow us to close this section with another story about

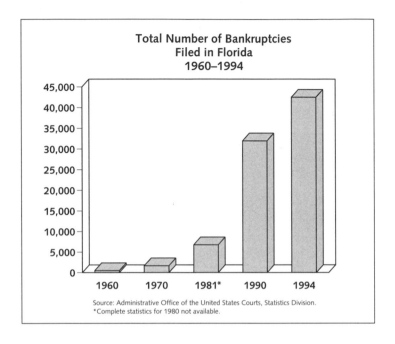

a foot injury. In May 1993, Vernon Henley and his new friend, Freddy, a guide dog, were at a shopping mall in Bradenton. Vernon Henley is blind and on this particular day, he was being taught how to move about with the assistance of his harnessed dog and guide dog instructor, Donald Muisener. The dog was being provided by Southeastern Guide Dogs, a charitable organization that trained Freddy and that provides other guide dogs to poor blind persons at no charge. As Henley and Freddy made their way through the crowded mall, shoppers moved out of the way. However, one particular woman decided to make a stand—literally. She just stood in her spot, watching Freddy and Henley approach and waiting to see if Freddy would guide his master around her. This is what she told other shoppers.

Freddy did as he was trained to do. He pulled away from Henley, signaling Henley to move around the woman. But Henley, who was just learning how to move about with the assistance of his dog, did not react quickly enough and he stepped on the woman's foot. As a result, her toe was fractured.

Sometime later, both the woman and her husband decided to sue Southeastern Guide Dogs for $160,000 in damages. The woman sued for her foot injury, and the husband sued for the loss of consortium that goes with being married to somebody with a foot injury. The husband claimed that entitled him to $80,000. They have alleged that this tragedy occurred because of the negligence of Southeastern Guide Dogs.

This charitable organization has taken a severe blow as a result of this first lawsuit ever against it. The lawsuit has caused Southeastern's insurance premiums to double and forced the school to spend money defending against the lawsuit. As a result of these costs, fewer dogs will go to help not just the visually impaired but the visually impaired who could not normally afford a Seeing Eye dog.[24] And who knows what other effects this type of lawsuit creates? If you are a good Samaritan thinking about starting your own charitable Seeing Eye dog business or any other charitable organization, you might read this and think twice. Is it really worth it? What will the costs of insurance be to protect against this? Can I afford to pay for somebody's failure to take responsibility?

So here we are with our culture in Florida, bracing ourselves against lawsuits and a variety of other social pathologies. There are so many opportunities these days to measure the character deficit in Florida that you often do not have to look very hard. This chapter has touched on only a few and some of the most obvious. From the tragedy of murder to the ridiculousness of some lawsuits, this is the behavior our children might just grow up to emulate. Nonetheless, we have a hopefulness for our future, and we believe in a number of years, we will see our indicators get better. If our families and communities do a better job of renewing character and virtue, we will see a change in our everyday response to, among other things, foot injuries.

# CHAPTER FOUR

# *Our Little Platoons*

CHANCES ARE THAT Chris Evert and Carlton Bailey never met. Though they lived thirty minutes from each other, they came from completely different worlds. Their experiences, their backgrounds, their communities, their glories and defeats were nothing alike. About the only thing Chris Evert and Carlton Bailey ever had in common was their status as newsworthy South Floridians. There was symbolic and poignant significance to the second week in July 1995 as the lives of these two strangers converged before us in our morning newspapers.

Chris Evert. Tennis champion. Ft. Lauderdale native. On July 16, Chris Evert reached the pinnacle of her career. She was inducted into the International Tennis Hall of Fame in Newport, Rhode Island. The induction was a triumphant finale to her sixteen years as a tennis professional. She was only the sixth player to be unanimously elected to the hall. During her career, she had won the Australian Open two times, Wimbledon three times, the U.S. Open six times and the French Open seven times. She was ranked number one for seven years and named the "Greatest Woman Athlete of the Last 25 Years" by the Women's Sports Foundation. Yet for all the pomp and ceremony that went with her induction, the true honors went to her family. Looking at her family, sitting courtside at the Hall of Fame and taking up fifteen chairs, Chris Evert said, "I just wanted to say this is for you. You are why I am up here right now."[1]

Chris Evert's home life not only spurred her career but also enhanced it. She grew up in a modest home in a modest community in Ft. Lauderdale. Her house was near the public Holiday Park tennis courts, where her father, Jimmy, worked and taught her how to play tennis. At age sixteen, she reached the semifinals of the U.S. Open. *Time* magazine followed her through the halls of St. Thomas Aquinas, where she went to high school. Yet she did not let it go to her head and she did not have a silver spoon childhood. Just one of five children, she was never singled out by her parents for her accomplishments. She still had chores; she still had to go to school. Evert said, "Other things—school and church and family—were still more important than tennis. That was the way my parents brought us up."[2] Her mother, Colette, would travel with Chris to the tournaments since her father did not like to travel. But even if her parents were not present, their support was always there. And unlike many of the overbearing parents of young athletes today, her parents always "had the knack of never putting pressure" on her.[3]

A few days before Chris Evert's induction ceremony,

another Floridian, eighteen-year-old Carlton Bailey, was shot to death on a steamy summer night in Carol City by three men wearing ski masks and wielding assault rifles. Though Bailey was not as well known as Chris Evert, in his short life he, too, had gained national exposure. When he was thirteen years old, Carlton Bailey became one of the youngest persons ever charged with murder in Dade County. This distinction made him the subject of a story on CBS's *60 Minutes* and in *Time* magazine, and a national symbol of teen violence. In 1988, Bailey shot his thirteen-year-old playmate through the heart because the playmate had put Bailey in an embarrassing headlock. Although Bailey was only thirteen, he had already been arrested seven times. According to *The Miami Herald*, his first arrest came when he was ten years old. It was for armed robbery.[4]

Shortly after Bailey's violent death, *The Miami Herald* reported that he "grew up in a fatalistic culture where guns rule."[5] This was true. Carlton Bailey's upbringing couldn't have been more different from Chris Evert's. Bailey grew up in north central Dade County. When Bailey was only four years old, his father was murdered over fifty cents. His mother was a drug addict and, court records show, would take her oldest boys with her when she went to get high on heroin. A social worker said that the family ate out of garbage cans. When Bailey was fourteen years old, his mother died. Later, one of his brothers shot and killed another brother by accident. After Bailey killed his playmate, his life was spent going into and out of halfway houses, youth halls and work camps—many in other parts of the state. When he was in Miami, he would live with his grandfather. Those who knew Carlton Bailey said he had a vicious temper, was cold-blooded and refused discipline. However, they said that as of late he was trying to get his life together, earn a high school equivalency degree and find employment as a construction worker. In May, Bailey witnessed a shooting during a crack buy that had gone sour. Police thought Bailey was involved, but he agreed to testify for the state against the shooter. That was until his conspicuous death on July 12, 1995.[6]

We are neither psychologists nor sociologists, but the lives of Chris Evert and Carlton Bailey strike us as the best and the worst in our society. Chris Evert's world centered around a solid, stable, supportive family, and she credited her success to that unit. Carlton Bailey did not have a stable family structure to support and nurture him. When his family structure did crumble, Carlton Bailey had no community to serve as surrogate. Instead, he became a child of the state. His home became the state institution, whether it was a halfway house or a jail. Maybe Chris Evert would still have become a great tennis success with a broken family, and maybe Carlton Bailey would have killed and died on the streets of Miami with a supportive two-parent family. But the statistics suggest that Bailey started with one major strike against him when he lost his father. According to the U.S. Department of Health and Human Services, 70 percent of all juveniles in long-term correctional facilities did not live with their fathers growing up.[7]

The family and the community are small civilizations in and of themselves. Society, family and community, as social units, all work to sustain their existence. And whether through laws or customs or values, each unit creates certain rules to carry out that purpose. But it is the last two, family and community, that teach our children how to respect the rules and laws of society. A child must learn to perpetuate a family and community before he can learn to maintain a society. The family and community are the training grounds for a child before he or she can venture into society as a good citizen. If a child does not learn to respect his family members and members of the community, how can we expect him to respect the multitudes of strangers who comprise our larger social structure? If Carlton Bailey was capable of shooting a playmate through the heart because of a simple headlock, why would he hesitate to shoot either you or me for money or to prove his manhood? It is the same reason why when Bailey was arrested for the murder of his playmate, he fell asleep in the squad car on the way to the police station. He had never learned empathy or self-control or respect for others in our society. On that night in Miami five years ago, he just could not comprehend the magnitude of his conduct.

Two centuries ago, Edmund Burke so perfectly wrote, *"To be attached to the subdivision, to love the little platoon we belong to in society, is the first principle, the germ as it were, of public affections. It is the first link in the series by which we proceed towards a love to our country and to mankind."*[8] The little platoon that Burke was referring to was one of many traditional local institutions. The family. The community. The school. The church. These were the means by which we once organized ourselves to solve problems.

The little platoons are the social anchors for our children. Those that do not have them are adrift. There is no moral compass to guide them. Children may eventually overcome not being associated with a little platoon, but it will be a difficult struggle.

Our families and communities teach the very basics about character and virtue. They are elementary schools for our children's moral education. We cannot expect our children to take on the geometric and algebraic moral dilemmas they will face in their lifetimes if they cannot sort out the basic "addition and subtraction" of ethical problems.

In this chapter, we look at the crises with our little platoons, the families and communities, in Florida and the rest of the nation. We trace the growing number of out of wedlock births, divorces, single-parent families and abortions over the last twenty to thirty years as well as the decline in some of our civic institutions, such as churches and synagogues and other traditional associations.

In Florida, our little platoons are under assault from all directions. *From one side,* the little platoons are attacked by individuals practicing a new form of individualism, asserting the "self" values over the common good of society. This attack is carried out in the name of individual rights. In deference to the "self," there are fewer men being fathers, fewer women getting married and fewer communities whose members will involve themselves in the struggle for perpetuation. For many, the community does not extend beyond their own living room. *From the other side,* the little platoons are beset by our bureaucratic centralized government. It is a government that rushes to usurp the roles of broken families and communities. The result of this is more money and manpower and regulations being inefficiently thrown at our social problems.[9] Right now, our society is one where the loudest voices in the debate over our social problems are the voices of individuals and the government, not families and communities. Therefore, individual rights and governmental excesses are each taken to the extreme.

But it is always the little platoons that are at the center. They maintain the high ground. Revitalizing our culture means nothing less than revitalizing the little platoons. Character and virtue will then diffuse from the center. We will have better individuals and better government.

It also means that we must restore the delicate balance between rights and responsibilities. Families, communities and individuals have certain fundamental rights. But for every fundamental right, there is a corresponding responsibility. The right to be free carries with it the responsibility of preserving that freedom. The right to conceive a child carries with it the responsibility for raising that child. We have the right to live happily and enjoy the benefits of a community or a neighborhood, but we cannot at the same time be hermits and ignore the problems in our community. Our society has its own moral ecosystem. Too many rights without responsibility disturb the ecosystem and endanger our existence.

During the Civil War outside a town in Pennsylvania called Gettysburg, a small regiment from Maine held a position on top of a hill known to locals as Little Round Top. With limited ammunition and few men, the regiment was told to hold the position at all costs. If the position was lost, Confederates could mount cannon on top of the hill and fire down on the Union line. Robert E. Lee's army could then strategically place itself between the Union forces and the Union capital, Washington, D.C.

Little did the Maine regiment know, but the thrust of the Confederate surge that day was to be directed at this hill. In wave after wave, the Confederates threw themselves at the hill, attacking this small Maine regiment. As the day wore on, the regiment first began to run out of ammunition and then men, nearly one third of their men down. Led by Colonel Joshua Chamberlain, a humble professor of rhetoric and modern languages at Bowdoin College, the regiment was ordered to fix bayonets. With no bullets to shoot, the regiment stunned everyone that day by charging down the hill into the advancing Confederates, causing a Rebel retreat and saving Little Round Top. Chamberlain's charge at Little Round Top has been considered the most pivotal moment of the most pivotal battle in the Civil War. Backs against the wall and nowhere to go but forward.

Current cultural indicators suggest we have come to our own civil society's Little Round Top. Our families and communities maintain the good position but are under severe attack. With little ammunition but lots of resolve, our local institutions must stem the tide of expanding government and individual rights without responsibility. The only way to maintain the position is to charge ahead. Our little platoons must move toward our social problems in order to cure them. It will take conviction and courage and a new attitude about how we conduct our own affairs in the family and community. But first our little platoons must fix their bayonets. They must be led by the most decent of society. Families and communities need to restore themselves so that they can restore character and virtue in our society. Just how far we are from this we shall see.

# The Crisis with Florida's Families

The most rudimentary and meaningful of the little platoons is the family. For most of us, it is the single most important institution. In fact, a survey of Americans shows that close to 95 percent of us say the family is very important in our lives.[10] For society, the family is important for the simple proposition that if parents fail, society fails.

First, it has come time for us to face up to the fact that the two-parent family is good for children. This should not be a controversial subject. It does not mean that single-parent families are bad or ineffectual. And it does not mean we should demean the heroic efforts of single parents who are trying to raise good, decent children or that we should ignore the fact that many single parents have the support of large extended families. But the truth is, as most single parents will tell you, the burden of raising a child on one's own, shouldering total and complete responsibility, is difficult work. Having a second supportive parent helps. Saying the two-parent family is good means only that having two supportive, nurturing parents is better than having one supportive, nurturing parent.

A two-parent family is good because the parents share some of the child-rearing pressure, and it is good for the children because it adds to the number of persons who can teach character, and generally makes it possible for at least one parent to be available for that child's daily or even hourly needs. The economic reality of today's society means that at least one parent, and probably both parents, will have to work. However, in the two-parent family, there is the added possibility that when Billy has a Little League game or Janie has an after-school project, probably one parent will be able to commit time to be there. Ask any mother or father and he will tell you that the biggest part of parenting is the "being there" part. In fact, the number-one reason why Americans think the family is getting weaker is that parents have less time to spend with their families. [11]

In Florida, and indeed in the rest of the country, the two-parent family is taking a beating. Between 1960 and 1990, the number of female-headed families in Florida has quadrupled. Nationally, the number of female-headed families has doubled. Even more significant is the rise in the number of single-parent families with minor children. In 1960, single-parent families accounted for only 11 percent of all families with minor children. In 1990, that number was 26.4 percent.

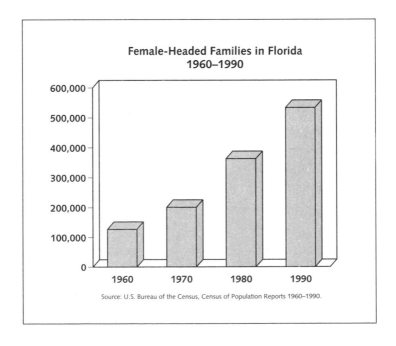

**Female-Headed Families in Florida 1960–1990**

Source: U.S. Bureau of the Census, Census of Population Reports 1960–1990.

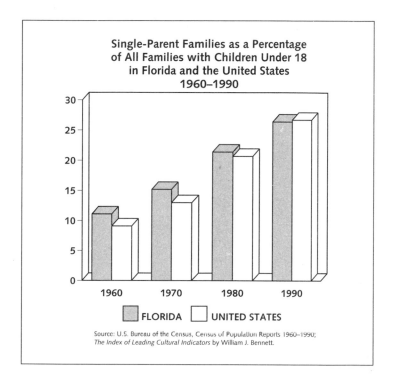

**Single-Parent Families as a Percentage
of All Families with Children Under 18
in Florida and the United States
1960–1990**

FLORIDA   UNITED STATES

Source: U.S. Bureau of the Census, Census of Population Reports 1960–1990;
*The Index of Leading Cultural Indicators* by William J. Bennett.

Recently, the major metropolitan areas of the United States were ranked according to the percent of all households headed by a single parent. Miami, Tampa, St. Petersburg and Ft. Lauderdale were all ranked in the top fifteen.[12] Why so many single-parent families in our state? The answer has a lot to do with our change in attitude toward parenting and marriage.

Responsible parenting begins with the pregnancy. However, in 1994, roughly 73,394 pregnancies were terminated by an abortion in the State of Florida. These abortions effectively reduced our birth rate by almost 40 percent.[13] Between 1973 and 1992, the total number of annual abortions in Florida nearly quadrupled. And today, more than one quarter of all pregnancies in

Florida will terminate in abortion. In 1973, that number was closer to 13 percent.

Concurrent with the increase in abortions has been a similar growth in out of wedlock births, disproving the notion that the former's availability will curb the latter's occurrence.

I believe in the right to life and am opposed to abortion. I know that there are those who disagree with me on this sensitive subject. However, I am confident that Floridians on both sides of the political debate can agree that more than seventy-three thousand abortions a year in our state is too many. I know of no person who thinks this number is too low and that we should have more abortions.

Such a shared vision strongly suggests that there is still *common* moral ground to this politically sensitive and often divisive issue. A woman's decision to have an abortion has a moral component to it and an accompanying sense of anguish. Abortion is not a right like the right to worship or the right to vote, which are pursued unconditionally. Even the strongest advocates of the pro-choice movement say that abortions should be legal, safe and *rare*. Abortion is not a right practiced with pride and enthusiasm, but with humility and reverence. Many of us caught up in the politics of the issue often choose to ignore what can amount to a lifetime full of painful "what ifs" for the women, some of them very young, who feel they must exercise this right. It is a great weight for any one person to handle.

But that should not negate the fact that abortion is a cultural indicator. Its growth is a reflection of our attitudes toward personal responsibility. While the political fight wages on, men and women of character should not be detracted from reaching a consensus that reducing the number of abortions is a worthy objective. Together, we need to do all we can to promote, encourage and reward responsible behavior so that fewer women will have to face the painful decision over whether to have an abortion. This would be a magnificent first step. Better education is another. Making adoption an easier alternative would bring profound joy to those desperately seeking children to love. These are noncontroversial steps on which we can all agree.

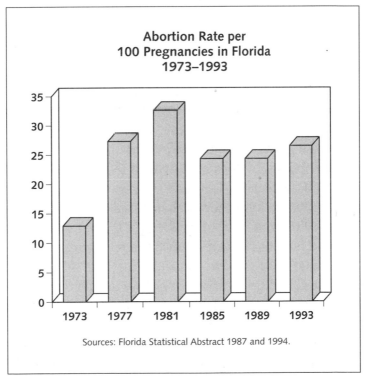

**Abortion Rate per 100 Pregnancies in Florida 1973–1993**

Sources: Florida Statistical Abstract 1987 and 1994.

Another indicator in Florida relating to parental responsibility is the growing absence of fathers in their children's lives. In Florida, as out of wedlock births and

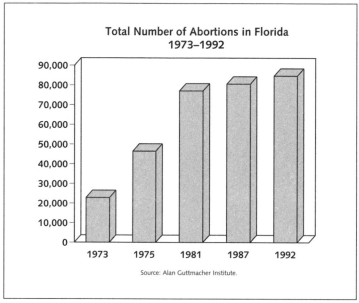

Total Number of Abortions in Florida 1973–1992

Source: Alan Guttmacher Institute.

divorces have risen, the institution of fatherhood has been replaced by a culture of fatherlessness. In 1990, only 61.7 percent of all children in the United States lived with their biological fathers. In 1960, that number was 82.4 percent.[14]

Historically, fathers have always had a unique role in society. Fatherhood has long been a symbol of authority, guidance and discipline, and for generations fathers have taught the same to their children. Yet all that the father has traditionally stood for is in danger of becoming just that—a symbol. The reality is that our nation is losing its respect for fatherhood. Author David Blankenhorn recently predicted that early into the second millennium, our nation will be characterized by two separate and unequal groups. He writes, "The primary fault line dividing the two groups will not be race, religion, class, education, or gender. It will be patri-

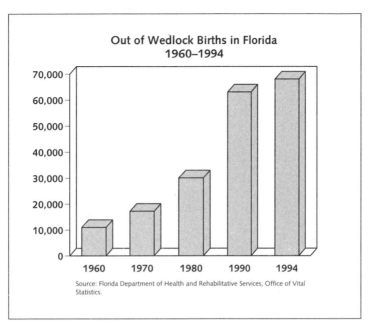

**Out of Wedlock Births in Florida 1960–1994**

Source: Florida Department of Health and Rehabilitative Services, Office of Vital Statistics.

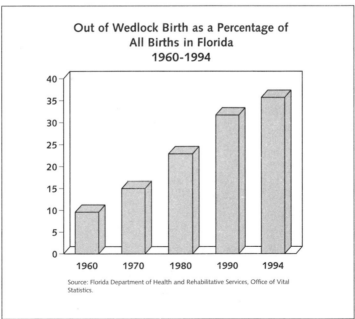

**Out of Wedlock Birth as a Percentage of All Births in Florida 1960-1994**

Source: Florida Department of Health and Rehabilitative Services, Office of Vital Statistics.

mony. One group will consist of those adults who grew up with the daily presence and provision of fathers. The other group will consist of those who did not."[15]

As the years have progressed, the numbers of persons in these two groups have already been moving steadily toward equilibrium. In 1960, the total number of children born to unwed mothers in Florida stood at 11,042, or roughly less than 10 percent of all live births. By 1994, the total number of children born to unwed mothers increased to 68,084, or more than 35 percent of all live births in Florida! In those thirty-four years alone, the total number of out of wedlock births in Florida increased by 517 percent.

The purpose of bringing up these high numbers is not to allocate blame to either the mother or the father. It is to make a point that we need to get fathers more involved in the lives of their own children. The incidence of fatherlessness is on the rise in our state, and it is spreading throughout all groups in our society, regardless of race, income or ethnic background. Over the past three decades and especially since 1980, the rise in the number of out of wedlock births has crossed racial lines. In 1960, only 2.8 percent of all white babies were born out of wedlock compared to 28 percent of all nonwhite babies. But in 1992, for the first time since the Florida Department of Health and Rehabilitative Services began keeping track of the number of out of wedlock births, the total number of white babies born out of wedlock surpassed the total number of nonwhite babies born out of wedlock. Today, more than 26 percent of all children born to white mothers are born out of wedlock compared to 65 percent among all nonwhite births.

The rise in out of wedlock births and divorces provides

perhaps the worst threat to the stability of our society. The effect fatherlessness has on both boys and girls, not to mention the rest of society, is daunting. Fatherlessness is the seedbed for many of our worst social problems. If it does not cause the social ills we are experiencing in crime, poverty or family breakdown, then certainly fatherlessness is a good indicator of which persons will be more likely to contribute to or be a part of these social ills. It is the critical element in Florida's character deficit.

For young boys, fatherlessness is an indicator of increasing juvenile violence. According to the U.S. Department of Health and Human Services, a large majority of all juveniles in long-term correctional facilities did not live with their fathers growing up.[16]

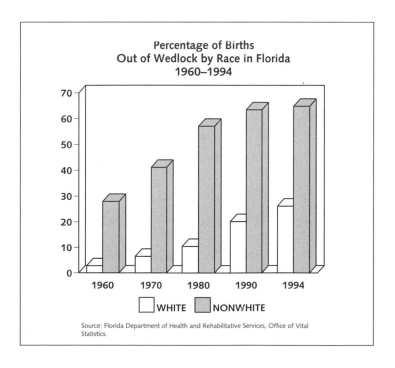

Percentage of Births
Out of Wedlock by Race in Florida
1960–1994

Source: Florida Department of Health and Rehabilitative Services, Office of Vital Statistics.

Similarly, a 1988 study found that the best predictor of the incidence of violent crime and burglary in a community was not race or income but the proportion of households without fathers.[17] One group in Florida studied crime levels in all fifty states and determined that "the number of single parent families in a state was found to have a significant correlation to crime levels—more than any other variables."[18] Those other variables include race, income and education. And, finally, the rise in the number of street gangs can also be traced to a fatherless society. Interviews with teenagers reveal that most join gangs because they have no other authority figures to look up to and because there is general approval and acceptance in gangs, something that fathers would normally provide.[19] Sadly, these gang members have something in common with another group of teenagers—computer hackers. Like the rise in gangs, the increase in the number of teenage computer hackers has been attributed to these kids' seeking to bond with other hackers in order to replace a missing or dysfunctional family.[20]

For young girls, there is a correlate effect of fatherlessness that can be measured by sexual activity and the rate of out of wedlock childbearing. Studies have shown that girls who grow up without fathers run a greater risk not only of adolescent childbearing but of divorce as well. According to one study of white families by a University of Wisconsin sociologist, daughters of single parents are 53 percent more likely to marry as teenagers and 92 percent more likely to dissolve their own marriages. Similarly, they are 111 percent more likely to have children as teenagers and 164 percent more likely to have a premarital birth.[21]

Fatherlessness is also an accurate indicator of other social problems, such as child poverty. In 1993, the U.S. Census Bureau determined that among children who lived with both parents, only 9 percent lived in poverty while among children who lived with only their mothers, the rate of poverty was almost 47 percent.[22] Other studies have shown that incidents of domestic violence and child sexual abuse occur more often among couples who are not married.[23]

Just as the pillars of motherhood, fatherhood and the two-parent family have continued to deteriorate in Florida, so too has the institution of marriage showed signs of disintegration. Although the number of divorces in Florida has apparently stabilized for the time being, divorce, a taboo concept in this state only a generation ago, is now very much woven into our social fabric.

At one time, long-lasting marriages were a distinguishing characteristic of our citizenry. In *Democracy in America*, Tocqueville wrote, "Certainly of all countries in the world America is the one in which the marriage tie is most respected and where the highest and truest conception of conjugal happiness has been conceived."[24] Hard to believe. In March 1995, the Council on Families in America concluded in its report *Marriage in America* that "for the average American, the probability that a marriage taking place today will end in divorce or permanent separation is calculated to be a staggering 60 percent."[25]

Marriage itself, like the two-parent family and fatherhood, has its benefits for all of civil society. Marriage creates our little platoons, the small civilizations. It brings two persons and their families together and links them for life. Siblings marry, and more families are brought into the network. More support and more cultural infrastructuring. But marriage serves other societal functions as well. Marriage legitimizes children. Marriage teaches us diplomacy and responsibility to others. And marriage provides children with the support structure and security needed to nurture healthy and virtuous adults.

Anthropologist David Murray has studied the institution of marriage in other cultures and found that when people stop marrying, their continuity as a culture is in jeopardy. Particularly interesting was his study of the Navajo Indians. For the Navajos, humane conduct in society depends upon the presence of kinsmen. According to Murray, the worst social characterization the Navajo can offer of a thoughtless person is the charge "He acts as if he has no relatives."[26] People without relatives feel no shame, and, simultaneously, they feel no honor. Marriage provides us relatives and fosters acceptable behavior.

But marriage is a dying institution, and divorce thrives. The indicators show that fewer persons are getting married today. The Census Bureau has already calculated that today, one in four Americans over the age of eighteen has never been married. However, in 1970, the number of Americans who had never been married was one in six. As fewer men and women are getting married, more men and women are living together. In fact, for many cohabitation has replaced marriage. But cohabitation does not create a platoon. Between 1980 and 1991, the number of couples choosing to live together rather than marry has increased by 80 percent.[27] And why not? It is a way of life that satisfies the self-serving characteristics of relationships while eschewing the corresponding responsibilities, such as commitment and faithfulness. In at least one study, research has revealed that 20 percent of all cohabiting women have had affairs as opposed to only 4 percent of women who are married.[28] Although this study did not survey the affairs of cohabiting men, it seems quite plausible that the results among cohabiting men would be at least the same.

Our lifestyle changes have affected divorce in our state. The total number of divorces in Florida has more than quadrupled since 1960. Thirty-five years ago, there were only 25.8 dissolutions per 100 new marriages in the United States. In 1992, there were 50 dissolutions per 100 new marriages. In Florida, divorce has always been a problem, but it is getting far worse. For every 10 new marriages, 6 will end in divorce. Since 1960, the

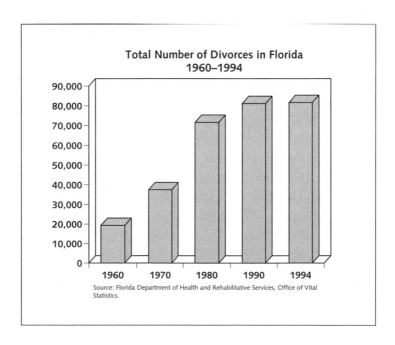

Total Number of Divorces in Florida 1960–1994

Source: Florida Department of Health and Rehabilitative Services, Office of Vital Statistics.

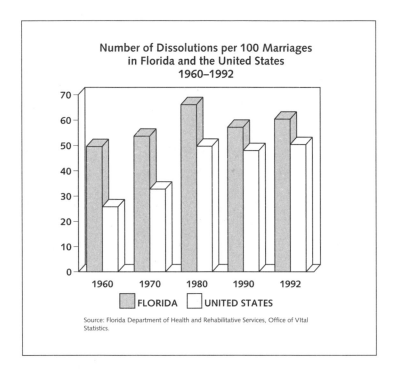

Number of Dissolutions per 100 Marriages
in Florida and the United States
1960–1992

FLORIDA   UNITED STATES

Source: Florida Department of Health and Rehabilitative Services, Office of Vital Statistics.

total number of marriages in Florida has increased by 263 percent. However, during that same period, the total number of divorces increased by 322 percent.

For many, marriage has come to be seen as one more constraint or commitment that clashes with individual choice and self-expression. In the early 1970s, most states, including Florida, adopted no-fault divorce laws, abolishing defenses to divorce. On the positive side, this law made it easier for women to escape violent marriages. On the negative side, it made it easier for men and women alike to escape their marital responsibilities. Today, each spouse has the unilateral right to terminate a marriage in Florida. As the number of states adopting no-fault divorce laws increased in the 1970s, so did the number of marriages ending in divorce. Before no-fault divorce, one had to go into court to prove abuse or alcoholism or adultery. Blame had to be assigned. Today, the standard for a divorce in Florida is "irretrievably broken." No questions asked. Somebody in the marriage is not happy or has found something more enticing.

When you put the number of our abortions, out of wedlock births and divorces together, the future of the traditional two-parent family looks grim in Florida. If you do some quick math, you find that a surprisingly small percentage of pregnancies in our state will culminate with a child raised to an age of majority in a two-parent family. Not accounting for pregnancies that ended in miscarriage, there were roughly 264,000 pregnancies in the State of Florida last year. Roughly 28 percent of them were terminated by abortion and 26 percent of the pregnancies resulted in out of wedlock births. Thus, approximately 46 percent of all pregnancies in Florida ended with a child's being born into a two-parent family. Now, considering that 60 percent of all marriages in Florida end in divorce, that *could* mean that only 18 percent of all children conceived in a given year will end up with two parents by the time they reach an age of majority. This number is not too promising for our future.

We need strong families in our society. We need more mothers and fathers. We need more marriages. Families are the models of character and virtue for our children. They teach self-governance, which means that the strength of our families is the strength of our state. As the nineteenth-century author William Thayer wrote, "As are families, so is society—If well ordered, well instructed, and well governed, they are the springs from which go forth the streams of national greatness and prosperity—of civil order and public happiness."[29]

## The Crisis with Florida's Communities

Virtue is rooted in our vital institutions. While the family is the most vital of all the little platoons, the community is no less important. The community is the next link in our character chain. By definition, community is the informal social structure that brings people together face-to-face through common interests and common geography. Community is manifested by the neighborhood, the church, the schoolhouse, civic associations—all bringing people together. As the primary organizing components of a community, these associations provide social support and instill and reinforce virtue. They also provide assistance to those who are in need of help and keep a sharp eye out for behavior within the community that threatens the welfare of the community. *Can* our communities affect overall behavior in our society? The answer is yes. But ask another set of questions. *Do* our communities affect behavior in our society? *Do* the communities teach virtue and character to our children? The answer to these questions has increasingly been no.

Our communities and local institutions are second-tier little platoons. How healthy are our churches and synagogues? How involved are we in our civic organizations and fraternal groups? What about volunteerism? To revive character and virtue, we must also rekindle the flames of civic awareness and participation.

Writing about the New England township, a long-standing pillar of community in America, Tocqueville said, "[T]he strength of free people resides in the local community. Local institutions are to liberty what primary schools are to science; they put it within the people's reach; they teach people to appreciate its peaceful enjoyment and accustom them to make use of it."[30]

In Florida, we do not have the strong history of the New England township. Our history has been one of growth and movement. It does us no good to romanticize the small-town way of life in the 1800s for it had a tendency to foster a separate and distinct set of advantages and disadvantages that would be difficult to replicate in this day and age.

Nor can we ask our urban populations and suburban middle class to become small towns. We must accept Florida's development and urbanization. Nine out of every ten of our residents live in an urban area.[31] Small towns are a dying breed in many parts of the state. We must accept the fact that urbanization and development mean that most of our communities blend into each other. Main Streets give way to strip malls. As I drive to work each morning, I pass through three separate communities—Kendall, South Miami and Coral Gables. Unless I note the subtle changes in the style of the street signs, I would have no idea that I was driving through separate communities.

While we should avoid getting into the business of small-town worship, we can still draw from the small town its better qualities and apply them to our own communities around the state. Foremost, it is the civic mindedness and participation often associated with the small-town way of life that is needed the most in our neighborhoods. We need to capture the small-town spirit of community and attachment. Recent studies suggest that the more engaged a community is in its civic affairs, the more likely it will experience successful outcomes in areas such as education, urban poverty, unemployment, the control of crime and drug abuse and health.[32] Civic engagement through organizations such as our churches and associations provides us with the best opportunity to apply our human capital in ways that can facilitate the coordination and cooperation necessary to solve common cultural ills.

Spirited communities do this by providing both the organization and enthusiasm needed to tackle our local problems. Just as strong families are better suited to teach character and virtue, so strong communities enable the people of character and virtue who live there to diffuse their spirit to all who would listen and learn. Community interaction helps to develop the "I" into the "we," enhancing our taste for collective benefits.[33]

This is a good point for me to make a confession. I love Japanese restaurants. There is one near my house that I frequent occasionally. You know the kind. You go to the restaurant with your wife and kids and they seat you in front of a big grill with other couples, other families. The chef comes out, juggles knives and flips little pieces of shrimp on your plate from four feet away. I enjoy the show, but I appreciate the set-up even more. The way the seating is tightly arranged in a U shape around the grill, you are just about forced to introduce yourself to others at the table and strike up a conversation. It is a coerced opportunity to meet people in your community. An oversimplified form of community interaction. You don't get that kind of experience in many other social settings. Not at McDonald's, not at Blockbuster Video. Believe it or not, the Japanese restaurant is a simple orchestrator of neighborliness. These kinds of places are good for any community.

Now for some bad news. Unlike our nation as a whole, Florida lacks the history or events that traditionally preserve our concern for the state and her communities. We have pride in our country as a result of events such as the Gulf War or the Olympics. In Texas, the Alamo fosters state pride from generation to generation. These kinds of events give people a sense of unity and community, and their effects are long-lasting. But Florida is different. In Florida, it seems as if our communities come together only to respond to a crisis. Hurricane Andrew and Hurricane Opal mobilized people to come together to help. I have also seen Florida communities come together to prevent a homeless shelter from being built in their area. It is a perceived crisis. Absent a crisis, however, to many Floridians community can be an unfamiliar and abstract concept. Few of us proudly boast abroad that we are Floridians. I was in Orlando when the Magic made it to the NBA finals in 1995. The civic pride was exhilarating. People in that part of the state wore their Orlando citizenship on their sleeves. It would be great if we could diffuse that same kind of spirit and pride throughout our state on a daily basis to attack our gravest social ills.

Florida's communities are not alone in this respect. In his book entitled *Trust: The Social Virtues & the Creation of Prosperity*, social scientist Francis Fukuyama observes that the delicate balance between individualism serving the "self" and community serving the "whole" has shifted dramatically in the United States over the past thirty or more years. Individualism now supplants community. For Fukuyama, this is in large part due to the decline in trust among people. As evidence, he cites a poll showing that in 1960, 58 percent of us felt we could trust most people. In 1993, that number had dwindled to 37 percent.[34]

If Fukuyama is correct and trust is a key ingredient to the strength of a community, then the best way to begin to develop the bonds of trust among people is to *know* the people of your community. We are more apt to help someone in need if we know who that someone is. That is why we are more comfortable giving money to a loved one in need than to a panhandler on the street. The one indicator that should concern us all is the answer to the question "Do you know your next-door neighbor?" In 1991, in response to a national poll, almost three quarters of us, 72 percent, did not know our own next-door neighbors.[35] In another survey, people were asked how often they spent a social evening with a neighbor. The number of those who answered "more than once a year" declined from 72 percent in 1974 to 61 percent in 1993.[36]

The poet Robert Frost once wrote that "good fences make good neighbors." There is truth to these words. However, good walls do not make good neighbors. Fences and walls are different. Walls block out absolutely. Fences you can see through or over. During the last thirty years, we have tried to both physically and mentally block out our neighbors. We have tried to distance ourselves from those parts of the community that do not concern our immediate interests.

In our own neighborhoods, we have unintentionally and intentionally built walls that divide us. Crime has forced us to value security more than community. Whole neighborhoods are now walled in, and we give them the delicate title "gated communities." The decline in the quality of public education means that our neighbor's child probably does not go to the same school as our own children, taking away something that neighbors traditionally had in common and adding another layer to the wall between us. Sidewalks and front porches have disappeared from our communities, meaning less of our leisure time is spent in plain view and within shouting distance of our neighbors.

When I was growing up in Houston, Texas, a small town of sorts back then, my parents let me ride my bicycle to school and back. We used to play in packs of kids. I was coeditor of a neighborhood newspaper and my brothers Marvin and Neil were reporters. We published a pet census counting all the animals in our neighborhood and printed sports scores from our local Little League teams. It was a real community. Back then, I knew all my neighbors—the Smithermans, the Vanderhoffs, the Swansons, the Kerrs, the Moores. There was neighborhoodwide supervision of our conduct. We did not engage in our day-to-day affairs in a vacuum. Instead, we lambs kept bumping up against the shepherds—there was always a neighbor's parent there to watch over us. Today, I confess that I do not know many of my own neighbors. Today, I would not let my own children ride their bicycles to school and back as I once did. In truth, many of us feel as one Orlando resident did when she wrote to *The Orlando Sentinel*, "I have to be honest: I'm afraid of my neighbor. My neighbor in need might be a drug addict who will break into my house once he knows where I live, or a homeless woman who might slice open my hand with a knife as I offer her $5 or some food."[37]

Before a community can effectively promote character and virtue to solve its ills, it must first know its neighbors and their concerns. And it must resist the urge to block neighbors out altogether. Time-honored institutions that have done much to bring communities together have been our churches and synagogues. Perhaps no other local institution does more to foster character and virtue among our citizenry than the church. Say what you will about the value of organized religion, the value of the church itself is true and multifaceted. In its simplest form, and for those who do not appreciate its religious aspects, the church brings people together and creates social relationships. Most churches do a fine job of alerting us to the problems and concerns in the community. In its more complex form, and for those who go to listen to its services and sermons, the church teaches compassion, faith, moral courage and civic responsibility. In either mode, it promotes character.

The church has always played a dominant role in our society. Our nation was founded on religious tolerance and we have never wavered from that proud tradition. However, there is evidence to suggest that over the last thirty years, the church has seen a modest decline in its influence. Since 1960, the percentage of our country's population identifying itself as church members has gone down. In 1960, almost 48 percent of us were church members. By 1990, the number of church members in the United States had dropped to 43 percent. According to another poll that asked people if they were members of a church or synagogue, the response was more favorable but the decline still evident. In 1965, 73 percent responded yes while in 1994, only about 67 percent responded favorably.[38]

Church attendance has declined as well. According to Gallup polls on religious attendance, the percent of persons who attended church or synagogue within the last seven days has declined substantially since 1958. In that year, 49 percent responded favorably to the question. In 1994, only 39 percent claimed to have attended church or synagogue within the last seven days.

While these numbers do not reflect massive swings in our attitudes toward the influence of church, it is still disturbing that they are on a downward slope, especially when we have come to a point where we need our churches and synagogues now more than ever. In Florida, limited statewide data have made it a little more difficult to piece together any kind of church

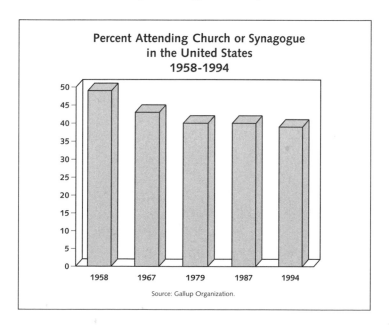

**Percent Attending Church or Synagogue in the United States 1958-1994**

Source: Gallup Organization.

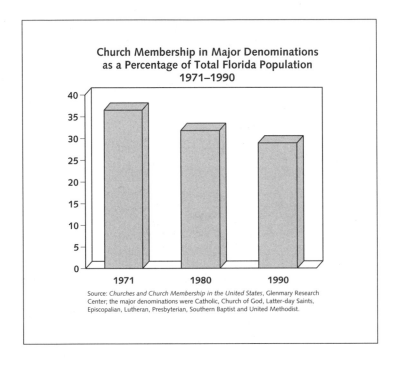

Church Membership in Major Denominations
as a Percentage of Total Florida Population
1971–1990

Source: *Churches and Church Membership in the United States*, Glenmary Research Center; the major denominations were Catholic, Church of God, Latter-day Saints, Episcopalian, Lutheran, Presbyterian, Southern Baptist and United Methodist.

attendance or membership trends. However, at least one research center has traced a variety of church membership in all the states from 1970 to 1990. Despite sporadic reporting by many denominations, we were able to compare membership in eight major denominations that reported their Florida membership rolls in 1970, 1980 and 1990. Those denominations were Catholics, Church of God, Latter-day Saints, Episcopalians, Lutherans, Presbyterians, Southern Baptists and United Methodists. Using these major denominations, we were able to come up with a "Dow Jones" of church membership in Florida, a gauge of how our churches are doing. And according to this highly unscientific method, the Dow Jones is on the decline. We came up with roughly the same decline in membership among these denominations in Florida as has occurred on a nationwide basis.

In 1970, 36.5 percent of Florida's population belonged to these eight denominations combined; by 1980, the number was only 31.8 percent. And in 1990, the number was down to 28.9 percent, indicating a decline in popularity of some of these more prominent churches. This downward shift occurred even with the inclusion of Catholics in our Dow Jones, a religion most widely embraced by many of our state's newest citizens, Hispanics.

Our churches and synagogues have not been the only local institutions to experience a decline in participation and membership. Traditional associations, such as the PTA, Red Cross, Boy Scouts and Girl Scouts, that have engaged parents and children and other people of a community have all seen decreased or fluctuating participation over the last few decades even as the general population continues to climb.

Harvard Professor Robert Putnam, the man who told us that participation in bowling leagues is down, recently conducted research to trace the decline of civic engagement in many of our traditional community associations. One of the most important of these associations is the PTA. Historically, the PTA played a vital role in the community by making the education of our children a communitywide interest. Our parents attended PTA meetings to find out how well or how poorly public schools were teaching their children. Parents came together as concerned citizens and neighbors when they felt that the schools were not doing the things they should. A show of force by parents could often change school policy. Over the years, however, participation has declined as more and more parents have been forced into the workplace. Fewer and fewer are finding the time to volunteer at the schools or to attend PTA meetings. Many have become disillusioned with the PTA as its mission has changed to one of all-out fund-raising. In conducting his research, Putnam found that participation in the PTA dropped from twelve million in 1964 to seven million in 1994, a decline of 71 percent.[39]

Putnam also looked at our traditional fraternal associations, such as the Elks, Shriners, Jaycees and Masons, as an indicator of civic engagement. He found that since 1959, membership has gone down 39 percent in the Masons. Since 1979, membership is off 44 percent in the Jaycees. Since 1979, membership has declined 27 percent in the Shriners and since 1979, membership in the Elks has gone down by 18 percent.[40]

The Red Cross, too, has had to consolidate its chapters and rally volunteers. In 1960, there were 3665 Red Cross chapters nationwide, with close to 2 million volunteers. By 1994, the number of Red Cross chapters dropped to 2413, with a volunteer base of less than 1.5 million, a decline of 52 percent in the number of chapters and almost 40 percent in the number of volunteers.

In the late 1800s, another popular local relief organization that was primarily a church was formed and is today commonly known as The Salvation Army. Local relief agencies in our communities such as The Salvation Army were important because, unlike government-sponsored public assistance programs, they taught those seeking help the virtues of responsibility and work. A long time ago, the army was famous not for its Christmastime bell ringers, but for its social relief

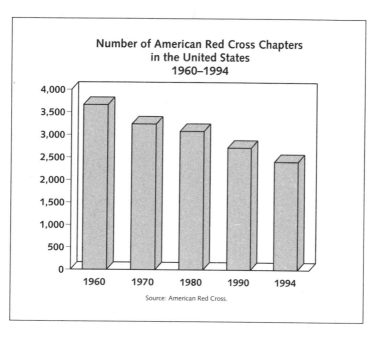

**Number of American Red Cross Chapters in the United States 1960–1994**

Source: American Red Cross.

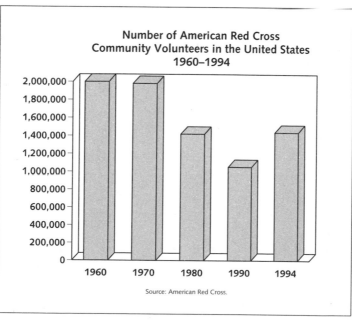

**Number of American Red Cross Community Volunteers in the United States 1960–1994**

Source: American Red Cross.

institutions that were based on "wood yards." At one time, those able-bodied persons in need of food or shelter who came to the centers were required to chop wood for their keep instead of taking something-for-nothing, hand-out welfare.[41] Similarly, at today's Salvation Army adult rehabilitation centers participants receive free shelter, food, counseling and "work therapy" but are required to sort used clothes, pick up donations and help with maintenance.[42] However, since 1960, the number of adult rehabilitation centers has declined from 125 to 119 in 1993. This number is up from the army's 1980 low point, when there were only 113 adult rehabilitation centers. Similarly, in 1970, in The Salvation Army's southern territory, which includes Florida, there were 746 social service units. In 1994, there were only 494 social service units, a decline of 51 percent.

Finally, and perhaps most disappointing, the Boy Scouts and Girl Scouts have shown declines in their membership rolls. In 1970, Boy Scout membership, not including adult members, was at 4,683,000 but by 1992, it had dropped to 4,150,000, a decline of 13 percent in overall membership. The Girl Scouts, the largest voluntary organization for girls in the world, is also pulling in fewer girls and young women. According to the Girl Scouts of America, total girl membership, not including adult members, in 1969 was at about 3.2 million and in 1994, it was a little more than 2.5 million. That is a 28 percent drop in the number of Girl Scouts.

In today's world of increased juvenile violence and child poverty, there is an extra sense of sorrow that goes with the decline in scout membership. Both organizations go a long way in fostering character and virtue.

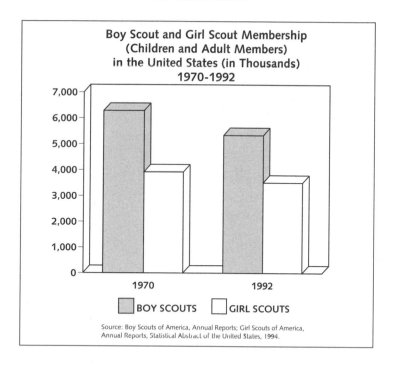

**Boy Scout and Girl Scout Membership
(Children and Adult Members)
in the United States (in Thousands)
1970-1992**

Source: Boy Scouts of America, Annual Reports; Girl Scouts of America, Annual Reports; Statistical Abstract of the United States, 1994.

Just listen to the Girl Scout Law. It states: "I will do my best to be honest, to be fair, to help where I am needed, to be cheerful, to be friendly and considerate, to be a sister to every Girl Scout, to respect authority, to use resources wisely, to protect and improve the world around me, and to show respect for myself and others through my words and actions." In that one sentence, the Girl Scouts manage to touch on just about every universal virtue in the book. The same goes for the Boy Scouts and the Scout Law. It states: "A Scout is trustworthy, loyal, helpful, friendly, courteous, kind, obedient, cheerful, thrifty, brave, clean and reverent." Nothing too controversial there, either. Furthermore, *The New York Times* reported recently that among men who were Scouts for at least five years, 33 percent of them had annual incomes of $50,000 or more compared to only 17 percent among non-Scouts.[43] So why the decline in membership in these organizations?

Part of the answer may lie in a poll the Boy Scouts commissioned that looked at the values of men and boys in America. Many responses in the survey were surprising coming from the men who are supposed to be teaching virtue and the boys who need to be taught. For example, the study found that two particular statements with which teenagers today do not strongly agree are: "Helping others should come before one's own interests" (only 28 percent agreed) and "Spending time with my family is important to me" (only 41 percent agreed). However, the responses from the men faired no better. To the question "What makes a good citizen?" 26 percent of all men answered "keeping physically fit" while only 12 percent answered "participate in youth-related organizations" or "volunteer time in the community"![44] When we ask ourselves why our communities are in the condition they are, it appears that we need look no further than ourselves. It is, as John Locke once said, that parents often wonder why the streams are so bitter "when they themselves have poisoned the fountain."[45]

In the end, it may be difficult to pinpoint with any accuracy why our local community organizations are stagnant. However, we do know this: The strength of our community organizations has been waning at precisely the same time our federal and state governments have been strengthening. This we shall see in the next chapter. When the community functions are taken over by government, people soon lose the sense of attachment and the urge to help one another. We lose our capacity for self-government.

# CHAPTER FIVE

# Abdication: Surrendering Self-Government

GOVERNMENT IN AND of itself is not an evil. A government of the people, by the people and for the people is not an evil. The truth is, without some semblance of government, our civil society would break down. It would be difficult to imagine a world with no police, no traffic lights or stop signs, no national defense to secure our borders. Few can doubt that government helps us to preserve a well-ordered society. It reflects our inherent need for stability and our respect for the rights and property of others.

And so, on September 17, 1787, with all the governments of the world and history before them, our Founding Fathers decided formally on democracy. It was a bold experiment, a government in which the supreme power would be vested *in the people* and exercised *directly* or *indirectly* by them through representation. It was a government created to perform those functions that individuals could not do by themselves—protect borders, negotiate treaties, coin money, provide for a postal service, stop counterfeiting, fix a standard for weights and measures. This was truly limited government, a government only as strong as its people would allow it to be.

In Florida as well, the government was to be limited. The preamble to Florida's Constitution lists as the functions of government "insure domestic tranquillity, maintain public order, and guarantee the equal civil and political rights of all." In both cases, we agreed to enter into a social contract, to surrender only a small portion of our freedom to our government in exchange for the protection of society against encroachments on our liberty and property. Jealous of our liberty, we would give only a little of our freedom.

In the beginning, we envisioned self-government. Our democracy was born out of a bloody eight-year war to free ourselves from an oppressive, intrusive and expansive government. We wanted to govern ourselves. As James Madison wrote of democracy in *The Federalist*, Number 39:

> It is evident that no other form [of government] would be reconcilable with the genius of the people of America; with the fundamental principles of the revolution; or with that honorable determination, which animates every votary of freedom, to rest all of our political experiments on the capacity of mankind for self-government.[1]

Yet more than two hundred years after Madison wrote these words, we find ourselves with a government that governs us now more than ever before: a swollen welfare state where government handouts and subsidies have become a right instead of a privilege; a public education system so bloated that change comes at a snail's pace when warp speed is required. Who is governing whom now? This is certainly not self-government.

## Like People, Like Government

In the previous chapters, we have seen how Florida's social problems continue to worsen or remain at their constant dismal levels. This has been coupled with the waning importance of the family and community in social problem solving. The third leg to this stool is government's role. It is no doubt increasing but what have we gained for all of this big government, all of these taxes, all of this spending, all of this bureaucracy?

For as much that has gone in, little has come out. Government has become our excuse for not addressing Florida's social problems ourselves. It serves as our civic crutch. Buddy MacKay told us earlier that government was the best means by which we have decided to organize ourselves to solve problems. I would argue instead that it has been the best means by which we have decided to defer responsibility. Leaders at the state and federal levels have been telling us for decades that government can cure our social ills. So we listened and we let government do it. And then there came a time when we just expected government to do it.

For thirty years, we have demanded more and more

of government without demanding more and more of ourselves. After all the promises of the Great Society, we figured that government could step in to fill the void. Let the Department of Health and Rehabilitative Services worry about the kids next door, let the schools teach the children right from wrong, let us create a Department of Education, let the judges dole out punishment to our wayward youths. As we abdicated responsibility, government was encouraged more often than not to address our social ills. Yet it could move only here and there, applying Band-Aids where surgery was needed, surgery that big government was incapable of performing. As a result, government failed in its primary functions enumerated by the founders; it became distracted from its first priorities such as public safety and order. In the final analysis, we the people broke the social contract; we failed to live up to the deal our Founding Fathers forged for us.

Today, we hear the horror stories. A Coral Springs woman takes her six-year-old daughter to a doctor to check on a minor infection. Shortly thereafter, the woman is arrested and jailed along with her husband because the doctor reports to the Department of Health and Rehabilitative Services that the little girl was infected with a venereal disease. Their daughter is then sent by HRS to a sexual abuse treatment facility and their other eighteen-month-old baby is put in foster care. The doctor's test turns out to be incorrect, and the Coral Springs couple endures another five months before it can regain custody of its infant children.[2] The anguish caused by stories like this should lead many of us to reflect on government's role in society. In 1994, pollster Frank Luntz asked people if they thought the government was "helping or hurting [our] ability to achieve the American Dream." Not surprisingly, 44 percent of the respondents thought that government was hurting their American Dream while only 16 percent thought it was helping.[3] The balance did not believe government was a factor in the American Dream.

If during these past thirty years the condition of our lot had improved, we might give pause to consider the benefits of bigger government. Government might have a bigger role in the American Dream. We might be writing a book called *Profiles in Bureaucracy*. But, unfortunately, our societal conditions have not improved. As more dollars and more manpower go into fueling the engines of government, we see less significant performance.

In 1843, Scottish philosopher Thomas Carlyle wrote that "in the long-run every Government is the exact symbol of its People, with their wisdom and unwisdom; we have to say, Like People like Government."[4] It is true that our government has done only that which we have allowed it to do. There exists an inverse relationship between self-government and government. The more we govern ourselves, the less government's role in our lives will be. Unfortunately, the opposite is just as true. The less we do for ourselves, our families, our loved ones and our communities, the more government does and the "more" that government does costs us dearly. The "mores" that will truly make things better off are more responsibility, more personal commitment and more involvement by our communities and families, more character in our lives. In other words, more effective self-government, the way it was meant to be. Only then will our state and federal governments play a useful supporting role in improving the human condition.

Consider the "more" that has been offered by government in the last few decades. Take education. Since 1972, the per-pupil expenditures for Florida's public school students increased by 442 percent per student. Yet during the same period of time, the average SAT score in Florida has actually declined by 62 points. Take poverty. Since 1960, expenditures in Florida for AFDC benefits have increased by 6061 percent, but now a greater percentage of children in Florida rely on those benefits year in and year out. Since 1986 alone, AFDC expenditures have increased by 300 percent while the percentage of children in poverty in Florida has climbed from 16.5 percent to almost 27 percent! Between 1970 and 1994, the child population in Florida has increased

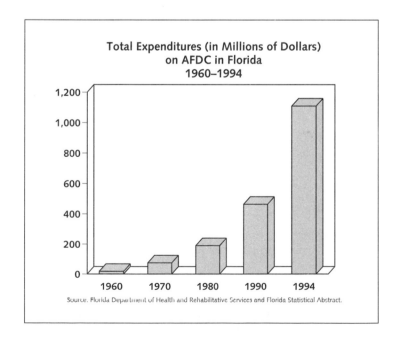

Total Expenditures (in Millions of Dollars) on AFDC in Florida 1960–1994

Source: Florida Department of Health and Rehabilitative Services and Florida Statistical Abstract.

only by roughly 53 percent while the number of children relying on AFDC has increased by 332 percent.

It is a shame that in today's political climate most people believe our level of commitment to curing a social ill can be judged solely by the amount of financing to be appropriated. As soon as funding for any social program is threatened, these people are quick to say So-and-so does not care, So-and-so has no compassion for our children. The tragedy in Florida is measuring compassion by public dollars spent. Compassionate people realize that excessive public financing has not helped the people who are most in need of help. Those seeking more innovative solutions to social problem solving are not people who want more crime, less intelligent children, more children in poverty. That is simply not the case. Just ask the profiles in character you will read about—many of whom are on the front lines, making people's lives better without government interference.

Times are changing. Fewer and fewer people are falling for rhetoric that says throwing money at problems will make them go away. In Broward County in the fall of 1995, citizens rejected a tax referendum by a margin of 71 percent to 29 percent. The measure called for a one-cent sales tax increase to generate revenue that would have gone for school improvements such as computers, buses and construction projects. Voters complained that they were already experiencing inefficient spending on education. A week before the Broward County referendum was rejected, Hillsborough and Pasco county residents rejected similar tax referendums. The wave of tax referendum rejections caused Palm Beach County to abort plans to put a tax referendum on the ballot that would have been voted on in the spring of 1996. Such sentiments are causing tremors in our capitals. In Washington and in Tallahassee, politicians are finally working to curtail government growth, to cut regulations, to trim down the departments and agencies if not eliminate them altogether. In a couple of years, believe it or not, we might even have a balanced federal budget.

# More Government in Florida

The growth of government in Florida and, conversely, our increased willingness to abdicate responsibility is measured by the input, the output and the size of our government. The indicators that follow show the disproportionate amount of money that has gone toward funding many of our social ills as well as the disproportionate amount of money and freedom we are required to turn over in the form of taxes and regulations to fuel our large bureaucracy.

### Spending
The first measure of the size of government is spending. Overall, social spending in Florida has grown more than any cultural indicator we have tracked so far.[5] In 1960, we were spending $84 million on social programs and welfare. By 1994, Florida's social services budget was that amount almost 52 times over—$4.4 billion for social services. Today, appropriations for social services now represent 38 percent of our total state budget.[6]

For those who wonder, the increases in spending are

## Total Social Spending (in Millions of Dollars) in Florida, General Revenue Only 1960–1994

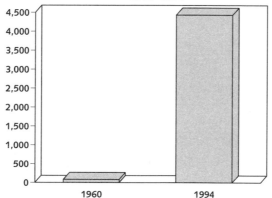

| | 1960 | 1994 |

Source: Florida Statistical Abstract and Florida's Ten-Year Summary of Appropriations Data.

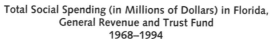

## Total Social Spending (in Millions of Dollars) in Florida, General Revenue and Trust Fund 1968–1994

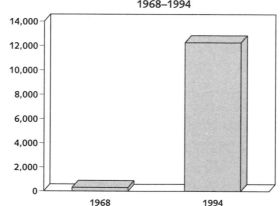

| | 1968 | 1994 |

Source: Florida's Ten-Year Summary of Appropriations Data.

not merely a reflection of our expanding population base. Both spending and the population have increased but not at the same rates. Since 1960, our state population has not quite tripled. However, it is nearly impossible to find a social program where spending has *only* tripled. In 1960, Florida spent $17 per person on social services. Today, Florida will spend upward of $319 per person for social services, even with our population increase. HRS now consumes more than 30 percent of our entire state budget while in 1968, it consumed a little more than 15 percent. In 1968, HRS had a budget of $306 million. Twenty-five years later, its budget stood at $9.8 *billion*. At that rate, in another twenty-five years, the HRS budget will be an incredible $313 billion! We cannot afford that.

No area of government demonstrates that our input far exceeds our output better than spending on education, specifically spending that has not gone into our classrooms or to our teachers. According to the National Center for Education Statistics, since 1972 total spending on public schools in Florida in constant 1994 dollars has increased by 130 percent. During the same period, our public school enrollment has increased by only 33 percent! As a result, our per-pupil expenditures have gone through the roof. In 1963, we were spending $372 per pupil in Florida's public schools. Today, we spend more than $4720 per pupil!

So where has all this spending gone? A little research shows that it is not going to our teachers and not going to the classroom. In fact, only fifty-two cents of the average dollar spent today on public education gets into the classroom.[7] Nonteacher per-pupil expenditures in Florida, such as salaries for education bureau-

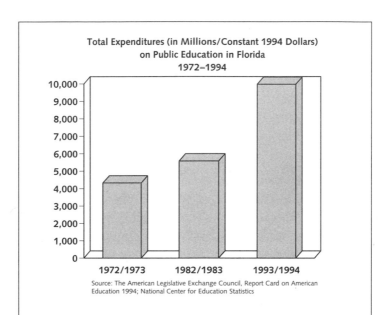

**Total Expenditures (in Millions/Constant 1994 Dollars) on Public Education in Florida 1972–1994**

Source: The American Legislative Exchange Council, Report Card on American Education 1994; National Center for Education Statistics

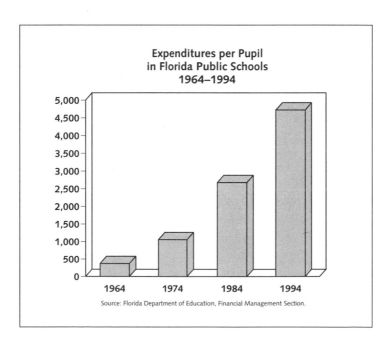

**Expenditures per Pupil in Florida Public Schools 1964–1994**

Source: Florida Department of Education, Financial Management Section.

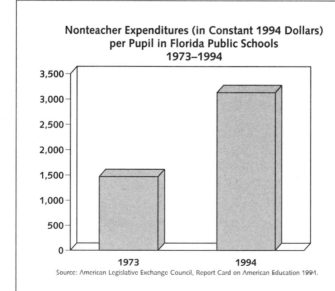

**Teacher Salaries as a Percentage
of Current School Expenditures in Florida
1973–1994**

Source: American Legislative Exchange Council, Report Card on American Education 1994:
National Center for Education Statistics and National Education Association.

**Nonteacher Expenditures (in Constant 1994 Dollars)
per Pupil in Florida Public Schools
1973–1994**

Source: American Legislative Exchange Council, Report Card on American Education 1994.

crats and administrators, have increased in constant 1994 dollars since 1972 by 113 percent. Teacher salaries as a percentage of our total public school expenditures actually dropped from 49 percent in 1972 to 36 percent in 1994.[8]

Of course, unabashed spending in our state has also increased in other areas where we are experiencing social ills. The war on poverty is a good example. In addition to the massive increase in AFDC expenditures in Florida, total expenditures on food stamps have increased by 7717 percent since 1971. Food stamps went from a $17 million program in 1971 to a $1.3 billion program in 1994. And it was recently reported that of this $1.3 billion, approximately $130 million in food stamps in Florida is lost to fraud.

Even the amount we spend to house our prisoners has increased dramatically. Measuring that cost in con-

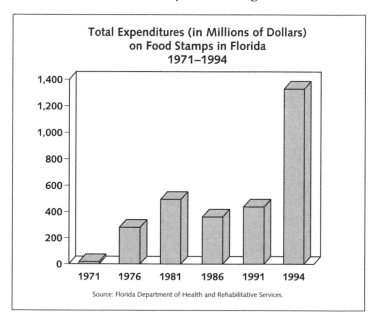

Total Expenditures (in Millions of Dollars) on Food Stamps in Florida 1971–1994

Source: Florida Department of Health and Rehabilitative Services.

stant 1990 dollars, we found that in 1960, the cost to house a prison inmate in Florida was $4952 but by 1990, we were spending $13,619 per inmate.

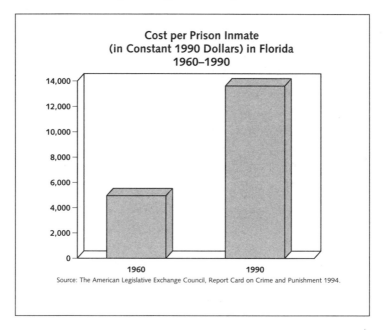

Of course, all of these indicators examine spending on programs for our students, the poor and the wards of the state. To be fair, responsibility and self-government require that we not turn a blind eye to programs that are considered by many to be corporate welfare. Let us say this, limited government does not mean limited for only one portion of society, one economic class. We cannot ask government to do less for the many while doing more for the few. Limited government is about the fair distribution of limited resources, meaning that as we criticize social spending for being no solution to our social problems, we should also criticize unnecessary corporate entitlements as no cure for our competitiveness problems. Creating barriers to competition and sanctuaries for profit is no answer. Many industries realize that they profit from a bigger, more involved government. Yet a return to limited self-government would not be complete without pushing these corporate snouts out of the public trough. Limiting the role of government must be a process that is rational, equitable and principled.

## Taxes, Bureaucracy and Regulations

Money is the key to growth in any government, and the more government has, the more control it can intentionally or unintentionally wrest from families and communities. Without the input, there would be less bureaucracy; there would be fewer regulations. The irony is that we willingly dole out the money to pay for the growing inefficiencies in government. Since 1977, Florida's state and local tax burden has increased almost six times over, from $5.6 billion to $36.8 billion. According to Florida TaxWatch, every single dollar each of us earned from January 1 to May 2 of this year went to pay taxes for the whole year. Though Florida does not have a state income tax, we are taxed in many other forms. Our general sales tax is among the highest in the nation. But we also have a separate selective sales tax on items such as alcohol, fuel, utilities, insurance and tobacco. Thirty-nine of our sixty-seven counties, most of them rural, have local option sales taxes, which include a 1 percent infrastructure tax or a 1 percent small county surtax. Florida also has a license tax, a documentary stamp tax and a corporate income tax. Local governments in Florida use the property tax as their weapon of choice. In the last four years alone, the

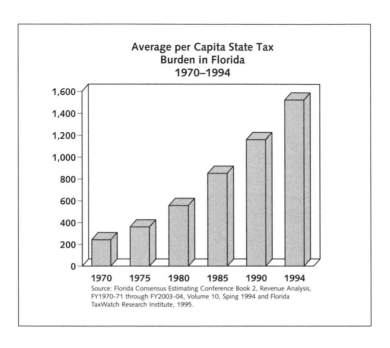

**Average per Capita State Tax Burden in Florida 1970–1994**

Source: Florida Consensus Estimating Conference Book 2, Revenue Analysis, FY1970-71 through FY2003-04, Volume 10, Sping 1994 and Florida TaxWatch Research Institute, 1995.

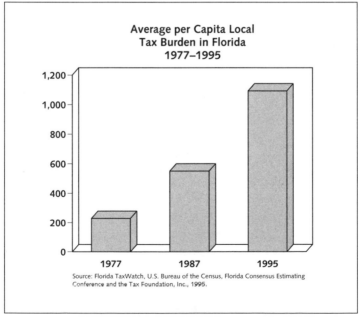

**Average per Capita Local Tax Burden in Florida 1977–1995**

Source: Florida TaxWatch, U.S. Bureau of the Census, Florida Consensus Estimating Conference and the Tax Foundation, Inc., 1995.

per capita tax burden from the property tax has increased by 45 percent.

In conjunction with the rise in taxes, between 1960 and 1992 the number of full-time state and local government employees in Florida increased by 287 percent as the state population increased only 183 percent. Our public school system has absorbed a large portion of this increase, but most of it comes in the form of administrative and support staff as opposed to teachers. Since 1965, the total staff in Florida's public schools has risen by 328 percent. Since 1972, total enrollment in Florida's public schools has increased by only 33 percent.[9]

Finally, the degree of control government exerts over our daily lives can also be measured by looking at our administrative code, the depository of our state regula-

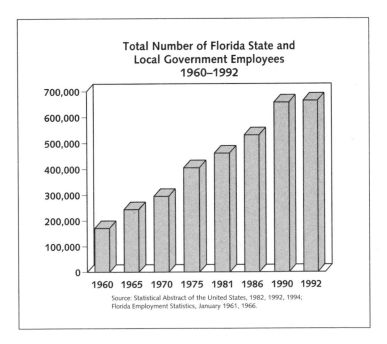

Total Number of Florida State and Local Government Employees 1960–1992

Source: Statistical Abstract of the United States, 1982, 1992, 1994; Florida Employment Statistics, January 1961, 1966.

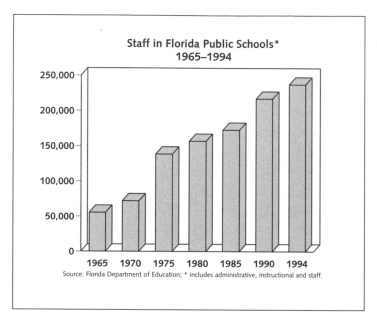

Staff in Florida Public Schools*
1965–1994

Source: Florida Department of Education; * includes administrative, instructional and staff.

tions. The Florida Administrative Code is home for many nonsensical regulations that provide minute details governing our day-to-day affairs. Some examples include rule 8D-5.004(b), which governs the content of brochures that may be displayed at Florida Welcome Centers. This rule tells us that the editorial content—such as photos, text and advertisements—of the brochures must comprise at least 60 percent of the brochure. Furthermore, rules 8D-5.005 and 8D-5.006 let us know that a brochure at a Florida Welcome Center should be vertical in design in order to stand upright in the display rack with the main message being in the upper third of the brochure. And if more than 5 percent of the brochure is dedicated to non-Florida material, that brochure will be ineligible for display at a Florida Welcome Center. Who enforces these rules and why are they important to Florida? The sheer volume in the increase of these types of regulations is astonishing. It is a failed philosophy of government that has caused the Florida Administrative Code to increase from roughly 9600 pages in 1981 to almost 25,000 pages in 1995. In 1995, we had 25 volumes!

No matter how we measure the growth of government, whether by spending or by taxes or by employment or by regulations, it all comes down to one thing: our expectations of what government can do and how much we will let it get away with. In 1788, James Madison wrote that in a government where men are no angels and angels do not govern men, the greatest difficulty lies in this: "first enable the government to control the governed; and in the next place, oblige it to control itself."[10] By entering into our social contract, by asking government to keep us secure in our lives and property and maintain our infrastructure, we have naturally ceded some degree of control to it. But by expecting it to cure all of society's ills, we have tacitly ignored the fact that our government no longer obliges to control itself.

# Rethinking the Role of Government in Florida

After all this big-government bashing, do I still personally believe government is not an evil? I do. Our state and local governments are full of honorable people with decent intentions who are sincere about helping others. My two years in Tallahassee as secretary of commerce taught me that our state has some of the most dedicated and talented public sector employees in the country. The failed philosophy of government we write about is not directed at their hard work. Neither does the failed philosophy of government question whether government can do good things. It can. The failed philosophy of government is that government can do all things. It cannot.

Government does have a role to play in our society, but that role will be a lot more effective and compassionate if and when the extraordinary demands placed on government are lessened. In his first inaugural address, Thomas Jefferson said that the sum of good government is

> [a] wise and frugal government, which shall restrain men from injuring one another, which shall leave them otherwise free to regulate their own pursuits of industry and improvement, and shall not take from the mouth of labor the bread it has earned.[11]

Good government is, therefore, grounded in its limitations. But as Jefferson noted, the first and most important responsibility of government is public safety and order. We have charged our federal government with protecting us against threats from abroad and from within through a standing army and militia. We have charged our state and local governments with protecting us against threats closer to home—in our neighborhoods and in our streets. Yet neither government does this so well. It cannot do so because we have not made public safety its primary sole responsibility. We have asked government to do so much more, and in doing so, we have spread it very thin. *Government has become distracted from its main functions.*

A good example involves the sentencing guidelines in our criminal justice system, evidence of a government that is miles wide and inches deep.

Sentencing guidelines in Florida are based on a point system. A convicted criminal gets points for the crimes committed and is not sent to prison until a minimum threshold of points is reached. Designed to keep the most violent offenders in our overcrowded jails, sentencing guidelines have effectively decriminalized many nonviolent offenses. While we can expect murderers and rapists to spend more time in prison, burglars, car thieves, white-collar criminals and drug abusers will go free unless they commit the crimes many times over. For example, under the current sentencing guideline system, which includes the changes made during the 1995 legislative session, a criminal will have had to have stolen ten thousand dollars' worth of goods at least ten times or have broken into a business at least ten times or have sold cocaine at least three times before he will face mandatory state prison time.[12]

The absurdity of the guidelines is further magnified by the rule that forces prosecutors to choose only one primary offense. A primary offense might carry a high point total, but any additional offenses will be deemed secondary and will earn only a couple of points. Consider the person who steals ten cars in one night. The first car stolen would get him 22 points, but the nine other cars would score only 3.6 points each. The guidelines require 52 points before a judge must sentence the criminal to state prison; therefore, it will not have been until our car thief has stolen his tenth car that he exceeds the 52-point threshold and faces mandatory prison time.[13]

A sentencing guideline system like this comes about because government is trying to do too many other things at the same time. We have not heeded Jefferson's advice that domestic tranquillity should be the first priority of government. Government should not be engaging in social engineering until government gets public safety and order right. The state needs more prisons and more prison beds to house our criminals. Taxpayers can understand having to pay for a more effective system of punishment and crime prevention.

But for the many other social ills we experience, the answer can no longer be more taxpayer money. We do not have it. *We must learn that spending more money or employing more bureaucrats to address our social problems is no reflection of our level of commitment to solving the problem. Rather, it is a reflection of the demand we place on government. It is a demand that government cannot, nor is equipped to, handle.* Governments do not raise children; governments do not teach hard work, responsibility, perseverance.

The answer to our social ills is self-government. Self-government will come only if we have a revival of character and virtue. That revival must come from within our families and communities. There is little that any government can do to encourage this revival, but returning responsibility to the people is a big step in the right direction. It will compel us to fall back on our inherent goodness and ingenuity.

At the same time, we must ask ourselves what the proper role of government should be. We must find the things government does well or should do well. In doing this, we should keep in mind three principles.

First, government is at its best when it is providing public order and safety, when it is preventing our encroachment upon one another, when it is building and maintaining roads and bridges. Floridians have wisely said in elections and in polls that they do not object to paying more for public safety, if we see this money being spent wisely. We must move toward letting government do these things first. These are the things that, as Lincoln said, individuals cannot do in their separate and individual capacities. It is imperative that government gets its primary responsibilities right before meddling in the social or corporate welfare business.

Second, government does have a role to play in the general welfare of its citizens. Public education and public assistance for those truly in need are legitimate and important areas for government involvement. However, doing the same thing over and over again and expecting a different result is foolish. Improved results will come only from structural change in which there is a shift in decision making away from bureaucrats and politicians who run government to a new social management team—volunteers in our communities, classroom teachers, parents and education and social entrepreneurs from within and outside the current system. Examples of this already-occurring resurgence include the charter school movement, neighborhood crime watches, the Big Brothers/Big Sisters program and 100 Black Men—an organization dedicated to helping restore paternity in our urban areas.

Third, too often in the past, we have created social policy without asking basic questions. What kind of behavior will this legislation encourage or discourage? How will a particular policy affect families and communities? Will it encourage individual responsibility or dependency? Will a particular policy provide effective assistance or will moneys be diverted to large bureaucracies? And should government even be involved in this kind of activity? We in Florida must ask these same basic questions before engaging in any more social legislation. Consider the following example: One welfare worker for HRS recently told a reporter that Florida devotes very little money to welfare programs. The article went on to note that only seven states spend less than Florida on welfare programs in relation to personal income in the state.[14] Those states included New Hampshire, Virginia, Kansas, Delaware, Colorado, Texas and Nevada. The implication appears to be that we should appropriate more for welfare programs. This response is typical. Has anybody found that because these states spend less than Florida in relation to personal income their problems with poverty are worse? If the question had been asked, you would find that New Hampshire has the least percentage of children in poverty in the entire nation, and all the other five states have a lesser percentage of its children living in poverty than Florida.[15] Conversely, did anybody bother to ask about the states that spend the most on welfare programs? Are those states curing their welfare ills? The cultural indicators suggest that these questions have really never been addressed in Florida.

The truest lesson to be learned from the cultural indicators is that human needs are best answered by other human beings and not by bureaucracies. If we can take anything from our recent social history, it is the need to impregnate our own civil society with the notion of small-scale personal involvement rather than grand-scale administered relief in the form of more government. And so we look to the profiles in character to teach us how to exercise self-government.

# CHAPTER SIX

# *The Profiles*
# *in Character*

I N THE PRECEDING chapters, we have spent a great deal of time discussing the many difficult problems facing Florida's families and communities. The only "profiles in character" discussed up to this point have been the many profiles of a society that has lost its moral bearings, profiles reflecting the loss of character— profiles in crime, profiles in irresponsibility, profiles in big government. If you have made it this far, you are no doubt feeling a bit depressed and eagerly anticipating solutions. How do we remedy the great social ills of our time? To whom can we turn in order to stem the rising tide of cultural discontent? How can we strengthen our own character and that of our children?

Character is not something that can be legislated. Government can do only so much to encourage good character. Yes, we can write laws to discourage divorce. We can write laws to strengthen child support enforcement and to improve adoption programs. We can write laws to make our criminal justice system more effective, more of a deterrent. We can even write laws to encourage more parental responsibility in our children's education. But laws do not make much of a difference if as individuals we do not respond in kind. Try as it might, government cannot force us to be good. We know of no law in the world that can make us more civil, more respectful, better human beings.

We have seen the danger in turning too often to government and the political process to remedy our problems. By way of analogy, the use and abuse of morphine in the medical profession illustrates this well. Morphine is a powerful and effective painkiller and is often prescribed by doctors for people who have had surgery. In small amounts, morphine helps ease the pain, but in large doses it becomes addictive and destructive. Morphine in such quantities can create dependency. Following surgery, doctors are careful to wean you off the morphine by reducing the amounts given and introducing you to less potent painkillers. In the short term, your pain increases while in the long term, you are better off because your body's natural painkillers kick in.

If we think of government as morphine to our social problem-solving scheme, then we can see how it has been overused. It is good in small doses to help ease the pain. But instead of small doses, we have learned to depend on government wholly to cure our social problems. We have not been sufficiently weaned off this drug. Because of this, many of our social problems are immune to remedy by legislation—the painkiller has become the problem. Whether we care to admit it or not, the answer lies in ourselves and not the laws. No pun intended, but it is a bitter pill to swallow.

There are good people in Florida who already understand the situation. They are liberals and conservatives, Republicans and Democrats, black and white, old and young. Profiles in character exist in every community across our peninsula; their stories are heroic and inspirational. Each of the fourteen profiles in character has in some way demonstrated the types of virtues that need to be instilled in each of us. One profile is about responsibility—a Florida Gator football player who goes back to the disadvantaged children living in the North Miami projects where he grew up to teach them the hard lessons he had to learn on his own. Another is about courage—a former prisoner of war from the Panhandle who spent years in a North Vietnamese camp, bravely facing torture at the hands of his enemies but refusing to waver from his love of country. One profile is about perseverance—a Seminole schoolboy who, at age twelve, ushered a food-for-the-homeless program through the Pinellas County public school system despite a wall of bureaucracy raised against him. One profile is about honesty— a wayward drifter in Orlando who while searching an empty lot for cigarette butts found a bag full of thirty thousand dollars in cash and, with only nine cents to his name, turned over the money to the police. There are many others as well.

Talk to the children in Florida and you will find that

they are searching for heroes and for role models to emulate. When asked who their role models are, these children do not fall back on the profiles in character. Our culture has not taught them to admire these people. Instead, the best that they can find are superstar athletes and millionaire entertainers. A recent sampling of students in Palm Beach and Broward counties turned up such heroes as Janet Jackson, Shaquille O'Neal, Sylvester Stallone and Rush Limbaugh.[1] We need to show the children that it may be all right to look to the stars but that there are role models much closer to home in our own towns and in our own families. They are silent heroes who know that money and fame are not vital components of character. Our children need to see and read about these good people doing good deeds, courageous people acting bravely, determined people demonstrating perseverance.

For our children and for ourselves, the profiles in character are a moral compass. *They* are the answer because they make us realize that *we* are the answer. We, too, can do what these people have done. It does not take athletic ability or a wonderful singing voice. It just takes the right amount of character. Government programs cannot be held up as role models for our children and communities with a sense of accomplishment in the same way that we may hold up these profiles in character. We can listen to the stories to see what makes the profiles the kind of people they are, learn about their upbringing and talk of their character to our children. If we are lucky, maybe some of their character will rub off on each of us. Maybe we will think of these people when we face adversity, when we think we have to be dishonest, when we consciously turn our backs on somebody who needs our help. This is how effective self-government begins.

At the same time, it is important to recognize that nobody is perfect. Even "Honest Abe" Lincoln found that folks who have no vices generally have very few virtues. We do not hold our profiles in character out as angels or saints. They do not float in the ether with immortals. They do not wear white wigs and found nations. We are certain each profile would admit to some of his or her own fallibility, and you will find some of them have already. Some of our profiles have spent a lifetime practicing good character; some have not. Good character is not about what percentage of your life you were truly good. It is not about keeping score. And it is never too late to turn the corner. Good character is about doing the right thing when called upon. It is about making the right choices in life. We ask that you consider this when reading these profiles.

Finally, we bring good news. Ours is a message of optimism. Florida continues to receive daily doses of human capital, our most precious resource. It is inspiring to hear that on a recent Saturday in South Florida almost one thousand legal immigrants stood in line merely for the chance to fill out their American citizenship applications. So many people in one day, eager to participate and contribute to our society! From the bright lights of Ocean Boulevard in South Beach to the quiet country store where you can get boiled peanuts in any Panhandle town, we find that we are not all that different. Though we may look different and speak differently, we want many of the same things. We want to feel safe in our homes. We want our children to be better educated. We want our marriages to work. We are bound by a common interest in promoting character and virtue in our society. Every day each of us has the opportunity to go and do something that will make us a profile in character in the eyes of a family member, a neighbor, a co-worker or even a stranger.

Bob Gibson, the great baseball pitcher for the St. Louis Cardinals, once wryly remarked, "Why do *I* have to be a role model for your kid? *You* be a model for your kid."[2] Gibson was right. We all should be role models for the kids; we all can be part of the restoration of character and virtue. But a character revolution will begin only when we have learned to improve ourselves. We need to strive through our own individual actions to be better people, to serve as profiles in character, so that when a child in the next generation looks up and says "I want to grow up to be just like you," we know that is a good thing.

# Dr. Pedro ("Joe") Greer, Jr.: Going Under the Bridges

## Miami, Florida

*The virtue of compassion is what moves many doctors to help heal the afflicted. But this virtue takes on even greater meaning when a doctor goes into the streets to find those who need help but who will not or cannot seek it. Dr. Joe Greer has spent much of his professional life caring for those whom nobody else will care for. He helps to heal the homeless and outcasts of our society, the many lost souls who live under the bridges and highways of the big city. For this work, Greer is a profile in compassion.*

In 1984, while working as a twenty-seven-year-old intern at Jackson Memorial Hospital in Miami, Dr. Joe Greer found himself treating a patient with a medical name tag around his wrist that simply read NO ADDRESS. The patient was suffering from an advanced stage of pulmonary tuberculosis. He was dying. Dr. Greer hated the thought of his patient's leaving this world all alone, so he made it a point to visit Miami's shelters to see if he could find out something about the man's family. One of the shelters visited by the doctor was the Camillus House for the Homeless. Says Greer, "My idea when I went to Camillus was not to start a clinic but to find this man's family because he was dying, and at the very least he had parents, maybe a sibling, spouse or children. I never found them. He died."

Today, Greer, a thirty-nine-year-old Miami liver specialist, reflects on that incident. Greer comments, "It was a little window into the world of poverty for me, since growing up in a middle-class family I had never been exposed to that. I had two questions: One, why is a person dying of a disease that's not only treatable but preventable, and two, what took him so long to come in? Something was wrong. Something wasn't working here. So there was no grand plan. To say the least, I get fired up for doing something. If I've got a cause, I get pumped up to do it." And do it he did.

In 1984, Joe Greer founded the Camillus Health Concern, a free downtown clinic for homeless men, women and children in the Miami area. When it first opened, the Health Concern received five hundred visits from the homeless. In 1994 alone, five hundred had become forty-five thousand visits in one year! More than forty volunteer doctors now man the clinic, treating Miami's homeless for respiratory infections, tuberculosis and AIDS. Many staff members are former homeless persons rehabilitated by Camillus House and the Health Concern.

Back in 1984, when the clinic was just getting started, it was all Joe Greer and one social worker. The "facilities" were a room at the Camillus House that was so small, the examination table blocked the bathroom door. Greer started the clinic by visiting the homeless who were living in flimsy cardboard cities set up underneath the major interstates and highways of Miami. He wanted to know what medical problems they were suffering from and he wanted to give them the confidence to come to the clinic. He was then, and still is today, a strange sight to see in a world of blight and danger. On many a balmy night, Dr. Greer, donning his white doctor's coat and with a stethoscope around his neck, is out making the rounds. He jumps, he climbs looking for patients. Most of the homeless already know who he is; he introduces himself to others and then vigorously questions them about his or her medical history. Greer is a street doctor making house calls to the homeless.

For Greer, the homeless problem is rooted in the lack of education, the breakdown of the family unit and the lack of socialization skills, discipline and shame. As a result of these fundamental problems, the homeless turn to substance abuse.

Greer's long-term solution to poverty and homelessness includes an emphasis on discipline. He believes that society functions primarily through discipline. "If you don't get up and go to work, you don't have a job. If you don't pass a test, you don't go on to college. These are learned behaviors in society, and these are the things that have unfortunately been lost in the inner cities of this country and outside the inner cities, too." For Greer, discipline in America these days involves too much gray and not enough black and white. He believes shame through peer pressure has a role in discipline. "When it's not cool to go fooling around, dumping your wife, the mother of your kids, then people won't do it."

Joe Greer grew up in Miami in the early 1960s as a first generation American of Cuban Irish descent. He often jokes about his ancestors migrating from one poor Catholic island to another. He thought the Miami of the 1960s was great but believes that families are the big difference between the neighborhoods of Miami back then and the neighborhoods of today. "There is an aspect of material being more important than family.... People want more, more, more without realizing it will all come later. You don't need it all right now. If you are happy with nothing, you can be happy with everything. But everything will not bring you happiness."

Greer's family upbringing has been essential to his own development. He practices medicine with his father, whom he calls "the most ethical man I know," and says that his one advantage in life was "growing up the son of my mother and father." For Greer, the effort you put into your family, the choices that your family makes are vitally important. Greer has been married for fourteen years and has two children. His proudest achievement in life is being a father but he notes that fathering a child and being a father are not the same thing. "Fathering a child is an act; being a father is a commitment for life. Any male without medical disorders can father a child."

Says Greer, "The role of a parent is to prepare our children for life. Life is choice making. Kids learn choice making from their parents. They will learn from the example their parents set." Like his own father, Greer is committed to being there for his children. "When I am in my office, I can be interrupted only for my family, my children and my wife. I will never miss one of my children's birthdays or events, whether it's a play or sports or something else." He tells the story of being involved in Hillary Clinton's national health care task force, which was holding a big meeting at the White House that fell on his son's fifth birthday. Greer was told that he had to be there. His response: "Listen, we've had a Constitution for over two hundred years. Do you think my presence is going to make that much of a difference?"

Greer beams with pride at being a first generation American and says, "In America, I am the government." As a result, he believes lasting change occurs from below. "Policy is implemented at the upper level," he says. "Change occurs at the grassroots level. Any policy or plan is dependent on the people to implement it." Public health, he maintains, is a public/private effort. There are roles and responsibilities for each. He encourages young people to get involved at the grassroots level at an early age, as he did. When Greer was young, he would read to a poor inner city kid named Gary at an after-school house in South Miami. They would read the same book over and over again. Says Greer, "I learned more from him than I felt I ever taught him."

For his work with the homeless, Dr. Greer was honored in 1995 by *Newsweek* magazine as one of "America's Unsung Heroes." This award included a gala event at the Kennedy Center in Washington, D.C., where Julio Iglesias sang in his honor and Mariel Hemingway introduced him. He was also featured in *Time* magazine in 1994 as part of its "Fifty for the Future" edition, noting the most influential people in America under the age of forty. He appeared in *Time* next to computer software tycoon Bill Gates. But when Joe Greer thinks about success, and especially the success of Camillus Health Concern, he has mixed feelings. "The success of Camillus is a fairly sad commentary on society. What I have done is not discover a cure for any illness. [The success of Camillus] is dependent on the suffering of others. If there was no homelessness, we wouldn't be that successful. So the best thing would be if we became obsolete and unsuccessful in our arena. But the nice thing about the success of Camillus is seeing how truly compassionate people in our community are. And seeing people who really want to help. That's the nicest success."

# Colonel George E. ("Bud") Day: Courage for Country

*Ft. Walton Beach, Florida*

*The heart of courage has nothing to do with the person who feels no fear. There is nothing brave about rashness. Rather, courage is about that spirit in each one of us bent on subduing fear so that we may face what instinct tells us to shrink from. The story of Colonel George E. ("Bud") Day is about one of our most revered virtues. It is the story of a man the Air Force calls the most decorated soldier in the nation since General Douglas MacArthur.*

"Courage, Jesus, please give me courage." United States Air Force Major George Day breathed this quick prayer as he was dragged into the Chicken Coop, a concrete torture chamber located within the walls of the Hanoi Hilton, the infamous North Vietnamese prison. He saw brown slimy patches on the floor— blood of American soldiers that had been beaten out of them in this very chamber. The North Vietnamese interrogator, called Goldie by the American POWs, stuffed a towel into Bud Day's mouth to stifle his screams. Another guard forced Day's feet into a pair of U-bolt traveling irons that were padlocked to the floor. Day was then ordered to drop his trousers and his hands were locked into a set of figure-eight screw-down manacles that instantly bit into his flesh. Then he was forced to lie facedown on the damp and cold concrete floor.

Given one last chance for a reprieve, Day was asked by Goldie to give a full report on the POWs' communication activities. Major Day refused. Guards who had been standing against the opposite wall with fan belts were then given the nod by Goldie and they raced toward Day, screaming to create an atmosphere of terror. They leaped high into the air, giving them the momentum to come down hard with their whips against Day's naked back and buttocks. In between beatings, Goldie would ask Day if he was ready to talk. Again and again, Day refused. The loud whacks soon changed into cruel splats as the whips ripped into his swollen tissue. Before long, each stroke produced a shower of blood, adding to the brown patches on the floor. But Day continued to resist. When night came, the guards left, but untied his hands and posted a man at the door to supervise one of the most hated tortures of all—"the kneeling."

With his arms stretched out in the air above him, Day was forced to kneel all night long on the hard, rough ground. If he fell, the guard's bayonet forced him back upright. The concrete began to wear bloody holes in his kneecaps and his joints swelled up to the size of volleyballs. At dawn, the beatings commenced once again. Day estimates that he received more than three hundred lashes during the whipping sessions. His mind wandered. The daytime beatings and nighttime kneelings caused him to hallucinate. On the fourth day of torture, his body rebelled. Day agreed to confess.

He made up lies about committees that the American prisoners had organized for the purpose of escape. Goldie appeared to be satisfied and went to his headquarters with the confession, leaving Day to himself. But Day began to fear that his false confession would lead to the torture of many of his comrades, who would be unable to corroborate his story. Major Day spent the night praying for more courage.

On the morning of the fifth day, Goldie entered the chamber. Day boldly told his tormentor that everything said in the confession was a lie. Goldie's rage overflowed. Day was ordered to drop his pants again and a new guard entered with a fresh fan belt. This time, Day was flipped onto his back. Beatings began anew on his chest and stomach. By noon, a blood vessel in Day's stomach had ruptured and he began to vomit blood and bile all over the floor. The rest of his bodily systems gave out on him, alarming the guards. The point of maximum torture had been reached; anything more would have killed this prisoner. The beatings subsided in the days to follow as Goldie was restricted by his commanders to giving Day only six to nine lashes daily. This was nothing compared to his previous five days in the Chicken Coop. Relying on the courage of a thousand men, Major Day had survived this ordeal.

The story of Bud Day is the story of a modern-day American hero. Born and raised in Sioux City, Iowa, by parents who were committed to the American Dream, Day's childhood years were spent amid a loving family that taught him generosity and the importance of education. Day grew up during the Great Depression. He recalls how hard it was for his parents to provide for him. His mother would make all their clothing, except for the big winter coats. Yet the lack of wealth did not detract from the moral riches Day's parents were able to pass on to him. Attending church was mandatory for Day and his sister. Inside the church walls, Day listened to the moral lessons from the Bible and then went into a community that conscientiously practiced them.

Day recalls his mother's strong sense of generosity. Whole families were migrating to California to find work and as they passed through Iowa with no earthly possessions, Day's mother would feed them, even if it meant going a little hungry themselves. Day was also shaped by a voracious love of reading. The books and magazines he read were a way to escape the drudgery and hard work of farm life during the Depression. However, reading also aroused his intellectual curiosity and reaffirmed many of the ideals that would guide him throughout his life. He read stories about his heroes George Washington and Abraham Lincoln.

Bud Day served in the Marine Corps during World War II and upon his return, he refocused on his education. Day graduated from Morningside College, a Methodist school in Sioux City, and then went on to get his law degree at the University of South Dakota. He married a next-door neighbor, Doris, from Sioux City and they adopted four children. As the Korean War commenced, Day decided to join the Air Force and learn how to fly fighter jets. He served two tours of duty in Korea. On the eve of the Vietnam War, Bud Day was one of the most experienced fighter pilots in the world.

In Vietnam, he flew an F-100 Misty jet, a sleek plane that was used as a target spotter for the American bombers. The F-100s would fly at low altitude searching for targets. When a target was spotted, the pilot would fire a smoke rocket into the general area as a signal to the bombers and other jets. As an F-100 pilot, Day would often be in the air seventeen or eighteen hours a day. On August 26, 1967, after making a pass at a confirmed missile site, his plane was hit. Day sought to gain control of the aircraft, but it was no use. The nose of the jet dipped, creating a massive negative G force in the cockpit. The faces of Day and his copilot were banged against the jet's canopy. Finally, Day pulled the ejection handle. His right arm had been broken in three places after hitting the side of the cockpit during ejection, his knee was severely twisted and his oxygen mask had mangled his right eye during the plane's nose dive. Day was captured by North Vietnamese almost instantly.

For six long years, Day lived the life of a prisoner. A man already in his forties, he was determined during his captivity to honor the Prisoner of War's Code of Conduct that all military personnel had to memorize. It required that a prisoner do nothing to aid the enemy and that escape be a priority. To many folks back in the States, Day's conduct would have been considered stubborn. To a man fiercely loyal to his country and its ideals, it was pure courage.

Early during his imprisonment, Day feigned massive injuries from the ejection. The guards began to get lax around him, and Day was able to escape. Surviving off live frogs and strange berries, he spent two weeks in the jungle, braving B-52 bomb drops and near encounters with the enemy. By the second week of his escape, fatigue and the loss of blood from his broken arm rendered Day mentally and physically incapacitated. He staggered almost naked through the jungle, talking to himself incoherently. Finally, he was spotted by the North Vietnamese and shot through the left leg and hand as he tried to run.

Throughout his six years in the POW camps, Day often exercised the virtue of courage. Many times, it would lead to gruesome torturing. Other times, it would inspire his fellow prisoners. In 1971, the POWs ignored the warnings of their captors and held a church service among themselves. The leaders of the service were hauled away to face more torture. Day did the only thing he could. In protest, he sang the "Star-Spangled Banner" over and over again. Little by little, every prisoner in the camp joined in. They sang all night. It was the first time in years that some of these men had not existed in solitary confinement. The emotional release created by Day's bravery made him a legend. Fortunately, by March 1973, the war was coming to a close and Day was released.

Today, at age seventy, *Colonel* Bud Day lives in Ft. Walton Beach with Doris. He spends most of his time speaking to younger generations and helping others as a distinguished trial lawyer. The Days came to Ft. Walton in 1974, when he was assigned to Eglin Air Force Base. They instantly fell in love with the lifestyle of northwest Florida.

Day has received just about every honor and award possible, including the Congressional Medal of Honor, the Air Force Cross, the Distinguished Service Medal for Combat, the Silver Star, multiple Purple Hearts and the Vietnamese Medal of Honor. Yet despite all the accolades and medals, Day proudly boasts that his greatest accomplishment is that his family was able to remain intact and supportive all through the war, which is a credit to his role as a father and a husband. His experiences in Vietnam gave him a renewed perspective on life. They strengthened his own character by helping him to see the things that are truly important in a person's life. While many veterans bear the scars of Vietnam and feel disdain toward our country, Day still has an undying love for America and searches for ways to continue to serve.

He believes that young people need true heroes with whom to identify. For Day, character means "living by the moral virtues that don't erode or get compromised even when things get tough. Honesty is always honesty, courage is always courage and a virtue is always a virtue. If you follow these things in your life, you cannot go wrong." Day believes from his own life experiences that courage is about making a decision after weighing the consequences that might jeopardize one's own life or career or something important. In other words, courage is about the will to sacrifice something in order to stand for something.

As he reflects on the direction our country has taken since his days at the Hanoi Hilton, Colonel Day fears for his nation. He sees a culture in decline and too many taking for granted the bountiful offerings of our country. In his talks to young people, the old war hero advocates hard work and being true to one's principles as the best means to achieve success in a land with many opportunities. Colonel Day knows how precious the opportunities are; he almost laid down his life for them. His life is a testament to why courage matters.

# Lawrence Wright: Putting Kids on the Right Trak

## Gainesville, Florida

*He is one of the most charismatic leaders of the Florida Gator football team. He has been known to practice in a Florida State football helmet the week before the big game against the Seminoles just to fire up the other players. But there is another side to Lawrence Wright. Behind this tough-hitting, tough-talking athlete is a person who is concerned about the future of his community. He knows what the young kids in the mean streets of the inner cities are going through because he lived it himself. And he has made it. Now he wants to help others make it too. Lawrence Wright, at twenty-one years old, is a profile in character who demonstrates well the virtues of perseverance and responsibility.*

It is every college football player's dream to play in a bowl game on New Year's Day for the national championship. But when that is not possible, these same football players find it just as thrilling to play in a bowl game to dash the hopes of some other team contending for the number-one spot in college football. On New Year's Day 1994, the University of Florida Gators were ranked number eight in the country, and although they were not playing for the national championship, their opponents in the Sugar Bowl, the University of West Virginia Mountaineers, were. Going into the big game, the Mountaineers were undefeated and ranked number three in the nation. A victory over the Gators would make the Mountaineers the only team in the country with a perfect record and practically guarantee them a piece of the national championship. It was not to be.

In the second quarter of a tightly played contest, with the score tied at 7 to 7, West Virginia's star quarterback, Darren Studstill, dropped back to pass and threw the ball downfield looking to hit one of his wide receivers. Instead, his pass was intercepted by Lawrence Wright, at that time the Gators' backup free safety. A sports writer for *The Orlando Sentinel* wrote that what happened from there was a "pure spectacle." Wright ran full speed toward the right sideline and at the West Virginia 40 yard line ran out of room. Many West Virginia players thought the play was over on the sideline, that he had been forced out of bounds. But at the last possible second, Wright surprised everyone by reversing his direction and dashing back toward the middle of the field, weaving and picking his way through the West Virginia team until he reached the end zone unscathed for a touchdown. The fifty-two-yard interception return changed the momentum of the game and the Gators went on to dash the national championship dreams of the Mountaineers, winning 41–7. Gator Coach Steve Spurrier called Wright's run "the dangest thing I ever saw."

Today, Lawrence Wright is a twenty-one-year-old junior at the University of Florida and the starting strong safety for the nationally ranked Gators. He is widely regarded by his peers as the most ferocious and hardest hitting of the Florida defenders.

Week after week, he proves his football prowess on the field of play. One would think with an athletic résumé like this, Wright would have his sights set on playing professional football in the NFL, but he does not talk about the NFL like some of his other teammates. This twenty-one-year-old talks about his grade point average and wanting to graduate from college—not just graduate but graduate with honors. He scoffs at leaving college early for the big time. "You start a building, you don't want to stop in the middle of it." Lawrence Wright also talks about a mentor/educational program near and dear to his heart that he started in Miami for underprivileged inner city youths. It is called Right Trak. In his relatively short life, Wright has already earned profile status, not only by giving something back to his community through his efforts with these children but also by overcoming adversity in his own life and persevering to get to a point in his life where he is able to give something back.

Wright was born in one of the toughest sections of Miami known as Liberty City. As a youth, he was a self-proclaimed bully and a discipline problem. He says he was a pretty bad kid, then qualifies that statement, saying he was a real bad kid. "Lawrence Wright just did what Lawrence Wright wanted to do," he says with a grin. He was always getting into fights, had brushes with the law, was suspended from school, got kicked out of the Boys Club and was a straight F student. His parents separated when he was born, so he lived with his mother, Janice, and his grandfather. Wright was more than his mother could handle. At one point, he was sent north to live with his grandmother outside of Gainesville, but was sent back to Miami after a short period of time because he was too bad. Wright was headed down the wrong track, in a direction that many of his friends would go in the course of their lives. Today, Wright looks back and says that that part of his life was about making bad choices, choices that often put him in the wrong place at the wrong time.

To his credit, he never got into drugs or alcohol or joined the gangs that were becoming so common on the streets. "Lawrence Wright doing what Lawrence Wright wanted to do" meant that he did not need the street gang mechanism to support him. This was in some part because of his large size and his toughness. His size and toughness also made him a perfect candidate for football.

After the turbulent years of junior high, Lawrence Wright, the discipline problem and failed student, enrolled at North Miami High School and instantly became interested in football. He had finally found something he loved doing other than causing trouble. Football entailed competition, something that Wright never appreciated until he found this sport. He was so good in his sophomore year that he started for the varsity team while his other friends were playing junior varsity. But his coaches, including former Miami Dolphin All Pro Larry Ball, told him he would have to keep his grades up if he wanted to continue to play football. Unfortunately, Wright's competitive streak did not include a love for competing in the classroom. He had problems reading and could not make sense of the words found on the pages of his school books. To compensate, he would act up in class as a smoke screen for his reading problems. His teachers just wanted to get rid of this trouble maker. That was until his guidance counselor, Sue Edmiston, took an interest in him.

This relationship would change his life. Edmiston determined that Wright was suffering from dyslexia, a disability in which words appear all jumbled together to the reader. With special glasses and the help of Edmiston, he was able to raise his grade point average above the required minimum to play college football. At the same time, he continued to do big things on the playing field, earning All-Dade County honors and second team All-State honors. As a top recruit, he committed to play for the Miami Hurricanes. Wright was finally on his way to big time college football, but one more thing stood in his way: the Scholastic Aptitude Test.

In order to be eligible to play football at Division I colleges such as the University of Miami, Florida, or Florida State, the National Collegiate Athletic Association (NCAA) requires that a recruit score at least 700 on his SATs. For Wright, this would not be easy. He was already behind the learning curve. His dyslexia had not been discovered until his senior year. He was also aware that many football players were having other students take their SAT tests for them in an effort to get around the eligibility requirements. Wright chose not to go down that track. Instead, he looked at the SAT as a competitive thing, like football. He was beginning to find the competition he so loved in sports in his own academic life. He studied for the test every free moment he had. That meant studying every night and every weekend, after classes and five hours of football practice each day. Wright took the SAT at least three times, each time missing the threshold requirement. On his last attempt to reach 700, he scored a 690. Wright's dreams of college football were put on hold—ten points short.

He did not shake his fist at the world, nor did he give up. Instead, Lawrence Wright accepted this setback and looked for ways to improve himself. He decided to enroll at Valley Forge Military Academy, a prep school in Wayne, Pennsylvania. It was the farthest he had ever been from home in his life. Valley Forge was also all white, as he describes it. But the experience taught him something valuable—study skills. Wright focused even more on his academics. The discipline from the football field carried over into his school work. He remembers the tough teachers and strict military life. Often, he would stay up way beyond lights out just to study. In his year at Valley Forge, Wright led the football team to an 8-1 record but, more important, he raised his SAT score above the NCAA requirements. His final score was an 860—160 points higher than the 700 threshold that had so eluded him!

Wright was once again a big-time college football recruit, but this time he shocked all by signing to play for the Florida Gators instead of the Miami Hurricanes. He reasoned that he wanted to help a team win the national championship, and Miami had already won a few.

As soon as Wright set foot on the Gainesville campus, he knew he had to hit the books. He wanted to avoid "starting in a hole and ending in a hole." He talks admirably about Stephanie Lutton, his tutor at the university, who has helped him keep his grades up and his study skills honed. Wright's remarkable turn-around in the academic arena paid off. In his first year at Florida, he finished with a 3.06 grade point average, earning All-Southeastern Conference (All-SEC) academic honors. He had come a long way from his straight F days in high school. In his second year at Florida, Wright elevated his grade point average to a 3.25 and gained a second straight year on the All-SEC academic squad. This is the one feat he is most proud of.

But the Lawrence Wright story does not end there. His own personal success on the football field and in the classroom was not enough. It is what Wright has been able to do with this success off the field and out of the classroom that causes his fine character to shine through. After his freshman year at the University of Florida, Wright began to implement his vision of bettering his home turf in Miami. As Wright describes it, he started having dreams about little kids trying to figure out what they wanted to do with their lives. He was concerned with the kids in the Lincoln Field and James E. Scott projects back home and with the decisions they would have to face in the years ahead. Decisions that he had once faced. And Wright was determined to do something to help teach these kids about making the right choices in life. That was when Right Trak was born.

In the summer of 1994, Lawrence Wright, along with the help of his former guidance counselor, Sue Edmiston, started a privately funded summer camp for young boys in the fourth through ninth grades who lived in the housing projects. Wright drew up a prospectus for the camp, put together a budget, started his own nonprofit corporation and solicited donations from local business and community leaders. The purpose of the camp was to teach self-discipline and study skills, the things Wright had learned the hard way. In that first summer, Wright, along with some of his old high school friends, Earl Little and Marlin Barnes, who play football for the Miami Hurricanes, and Ricardo "Rock" Preston, a star running back for the Florida State Seminoles, went into the projects to recruit the first Right Trak class. They looked for kids who were primarily from single-parent families, kids who were having problems in school but kids who also had something good about them and who had not slipped too far into the bad elements of inner city life. They told the youngsters it would be a football camp.

When more than forty kids showed up, however, they found they were in store for something more than just football. In the morning, the kids had seminars and tutoring sessions and in the afternoon, they played football. Wright lectured them about "making the right choices." He pushed them on their study skills and preached about academics. He taught the kids to study in thirty-minute intervals, taking a break for fifteen minutes and then starting over again. Wright motivated them. By summer's end, the kids seemed to thrive on the message their real-life role model was teaching. Yet on the last day of the camp at graduation ceremonies, only four parents showed up. It was a big disappointment for all.

During the following football season, the graduates of Right Trak took a trip to Gainesville to watch Wright play in a football game. After the game, an exhausted Lawrence Wright went through all of the kids' report cards and met with each of them individually. Many of their report cards remained poor, and there were a lot of tears as their role model came down hard on them.

It was at that point that Wright realized he had to give the kids something more than just a summer camp. He needed to give them the means for bringing their grades up. So began the Right Trak tutoring program. With the help of Edmiston, once-a-week sessions were set up at North Miami High School, where the kids were taught study skills by honor society students, student athletes and members of the North Miami community. When Wright was in town, he would come and lecture. The program continues today.

Right Trak entered its second year this past summer. The first day of camp found Wright with forty-five kids in a field at North Miami High School in 90-plus-degree heat doing duck walks (a grueling exercise where you walk in a squatting position) with the kids for discipline. They repeated the drill over and over until they got it right. At times, the sessions seem like boot camp, but it is at those times that Wright stresses discipline. He makes all of the kids do pushups when one of them misbehaves. The kids complain and moan but eventually realize that they will not be rewarded with fun activities until they do as Wright says. He teaches them what he has learned—that "nothing is going to come easy. There is a challenge in everything."

Throughout the camp, Wright provided these youths with a broad range of experiences. They heard Marc Buoniconti of the Miami Project speak from his wheelchair, as well as Johnny Winters, a representative from Get Out And Live (GOAL), who is impaired by cerebral palsy, lecture on how they could overcome any of their obstacles. The kids visited North Shore Medical Center for a medical screening. They also had a workday at a law firm in downtown Miami. Says Wright,

"The idea was to get them out of the community and show them a different environment." Wright even planned a session called Rap Art, sponsored by an association of graphic designers, where the kids heard from various people who held jobs in the art industry, including a Disney artist, a professional photographer and a paper supplier. Afterward, the kids painted life-size pictures of themselves in the roles of what they wanted to be when they grew up. Their drawings included a doctor, a lawyer, a judge, an artist and Uncle Sam. "Everybody is not destined to be an academic success, but everyone has the skill to hold a job," says Wright. "I want to give these kids enough choices to become something. The more choices I can offer them, the more successful they will become. I have got to get these kids to believe in themselves and to show them how to make it through adversity."

Where parents and families have failed, Lawrence Wright and his other Right Trak counselors, with all their success on the football field, have come back to their community to lend a hand. They are young men who have stepped into the void in their neighborhoods and are taking responsibility for bettering society.

On the final day of camp last summer, Wright and the other counselors hosted a graduation/award ceremony. The counselors donned their game jerseys from their respective colleges. The kids all wore T-shirts that read DETERMINATION + MOTIVATION × ATTITUDE = SUCCESS. This year, about fifteen parents showed up. Wright passed out shiny gold medals to those kids who had demonstrated commitment by coming to every session of the camp. Some did not get gold medals. There were tears, but Wright did not buckle. He lectured them again about the importance of commitment. He told them that he had made a commitment to drive down from Gainesville every weekend to be there for them, and that they had committed to come to camp every weekend. Then each child who had a parent or relative at the ceremony presented that person with a flower and a promise to commit to improving themselves over the next year. Again, there were tears, tears among the parents and the kids as they looked in their parents' eyes and committed before the whole group to study more or not to do drugs. Wright admits that in the second year of Right Trak, attendance is up and grades are getting better, but the grades of these kids are still not where he wants them to be. He will keep on them. He will continue to lecture them about school and how "school is just like an everyday game of football—you have to prepare yourself." Wright is proud that what started out as just a dream and a summer camp for underprivileged youths today is a year-round tutoring and mentor program. He is also pleased that his family and friends are proud of him. "I've been bad for so long, I wanted to give them something to show others what a good person I have become."

Wright freely acknowledges that his life and the Right Trak are all about character. "Character is the trunk of a tree that everything branches from," he says. "Character is within us. There are many situations in your life that will be full of adversity. Character is what helps you build a tunnel underneath or bridge over that adversity. You have to learn how to resolve conflicts." But in a moment of humility, he is quick to point out that he has a long way to go with his own character. He concedes that he is not all good.

At the end of the 1995 football season, Lawrence Wright was named to the Southeastern Conference's "Good Works Team," which honors those who have demonstrated superior community service efforts. The team consists of one player from each Southeastern Conference school. But it is merely another award for Wright, who is still looking far into the future. For Lawrence Wright, Right Trak is just a manifestation of bigger things to come. Years down the road, Wright, a building construction major at Florida, sees himself as the owner of a general contracting business and would like to build a multipurpose center for the disadvantaged. The center would be a vocational school where people could learn all kinds of trade skills, such as plumbing, electrical or secretarial skills. It would have a tutorial aspect where kids would help other kids with their schoolwork. Day care and dental care would also be provided. Church services too. And, of course, those at the center could also enjoy sports. Then Wright envisions that he will be able to give many of the kids and teenagers from his center the opportunity to work for him. People from his community all working together. To get there, Wright knows he will have to make a sacrifice and work hard. But he has a strong personal belief in himself and what he can accomplish.

Wright is determined to make his dreams a reality. He recognizes that his own community has a long way to go. But Wright is not intimidated by adversity. He has experienced his own problems and has overcome much in his own life. He is a profile who knows the meaning of perseverance and of giving back to his community. He is a man who has a large family to care for.

So when you turn on your television sets on Saturday afternoons and see number 4 for the Florida Gators drilling another wide receiver or quarterback, remember that there are forty-five young boys back in Miami who are cheering, not for a great play but for a young man who cares for them and who has helped them to dream just a little of what they can be.

# David Levitt:
# The Story of David and Goliath

## Seminole, Florida

*At some point in our lives we have all experienced the frustration of bureaucracy, whether it is standing in a line to renew a driver's license, trying to obtain the necessary permits to build something in our own backyard or following the budget debates in the news. Chances are, if you have ever tried to fight this monster, you have lost. Many of us know from experience that challenging bureaucracy can be futile, so we surrender without a fight. This is a story about one boy's refusal to surrender and his dogged perseverance—a virtue he used to help implement a wonderful program for the hungry.*

Youthful ignorance is bliss. It provides our children with the will to do what they set their minds to sans the careful calculating that causes many of us older folk not to even try. At age eleven, David Levitt, a mere sixth grader, did not even know what the word "bureaucracy" meant. What Levitt did have, though, was a powerful idea rooted in the will to help the less fortunate.

It all started one Sunday morning in the spring of

1993 while Levitt was reading an article in *Parade Magazine* entitled "The Power of an Idea." The story was about a man in Kentucky named Stan Curtis, who founded a network of volunteers to transport donated food to hungry recipients. Curtis's program, called Harvest U.S.A., had grown through the years to become one of the largest such nonprofit organizations in the nation. Levitt was so intrigued by the story that he wondered if he could set up a chapter of Harvest U.S.A. in the Tampa Bay area. The good news, he soon found out, was that there was indeed such a chapter already in place, Tampa Bay Harvest.

In the weeks that followed, David and his mom met with the president of the local chapter to see how David could get involved. She provided them with all kinds of information about food donor programs. One particular program in Louisville, Kentucky, caught David's eye. It was called "Operation Food for Thought," a program that donated leftover food from the public school cafeterias in Louisville to the hungry. David's idea was simple—implement a similar program in conjunction with the Pinellas County school system whereby the leftover food would go to local soup kitchens.

David did not foresee any difficulty in carrying out this good idea. He first approached his school principal with the proposal. But with Pinellas County serving more than ninety thousand students in more than ninety schools, the principal told David there was just too much red tape involved to get a program like this off the ground. David was also told by school board officials that many people had made similar proposals only to be defeated by bureaucratic red tape. Nevertheless, David would not be discouraged. He was incredulous that such a worthy idea could be held up by a government created to help us.

So for the next few weeks, David did his homework. He gathered the ammunition that would be needed to push his program through whatever bureaucratic quagmires were ahead. He collected information from Tampa Bay Harvest, from the Kentucky Operation Food for Thought and researched the Florida Good Samaritan laws regarding food donations. He then wrote a report on the program, summarizing its goals and structure, packaged the information neatly and personally delivered his proposal to all seven members of the Pinellas County school board as well as the superintendent of schools.

While in the administration building where the school board members' offices were located, David was taken into an empty meeting room. Photographs of all the board members were hanging on the wall. As he looked at them he wondered how he was going to be able to sway these powerful people when so many before him had failed. He knew what he had to do.

During the following week, the eleven-year-old visited each school board member to personally push his proposal. Reactions to his efforts were favorable. On his twelfth birthday, David found himself standing before the Pinellas County school board in the very room he had been awed by only weeks before. His persistence and hard work had temporarily paid off. Unlike the others before him, the school board unanimously approved the proposal and referred it to the food services director so that details could be ironed out with the health department and the Florida

Department of Agriculture. David claimed his victory and said, "It just took a kid to make them see this matters." But the bureaucracy was only beginning to stir.

By late March 1994, roughly five months later, the program had yet to be implemented, and David was getting impatient with this thing called bureaucracy. Food was being wasted and people were going hungry, but few seemed to care. David enlisted the help of the president of Tampa Bay Harvest and found out that the holdup was with food services and the health department. There were problems on the government's end in drafting the required "hold harmless" agreements. Furthermore, nobody was letting any part of the food program go forward until airtight containers could be found and the school system's budget had no money to allocate for that purpose. This had been an existing problem that had not been brought to David's attention by any of the various governmental entities in the months following the school board presentation. Had David not inquired, the program might have just died there. But identifying the problem did not help matters. David was told that the responsibility for the containers had to be assumed by Tampa Bay Harvest, which operates on very limited funds. It was then that David's dream really appeared headed for a dusty death as a stack of paper on a shelf somewhere.

In his quest for airtight containers, David was on his own. He visited his local supermarket, writing down the addresses of the various container manufacturers that were on the boxes. He then sent letters to every company he could find that manufactured airtight containers. Publix sent him a one-hundred-dollar gift certificate to purchase containers, but that would not be enough for the massive amounts of food that would have to be transported. To his delight, Glad-Lock Company contacted David and sent him eight cases of storage bags. He was making progress. So impressed by David's idea, Glad-Lock soon increased its support by sending a pallet of containers to Tampa Bay Harvest and then committing to provide an ongoing supply.

Approximately one year after the sixth grader had gone before the school board, the first ten schools in Pinellas began donating their food to the volunteer transportation network. Today, eighty-two of the ninety-two schools send their leftover lunches to soup kitchens and local shelters. By the end of the 1994–1995 school year, Pinellas County had donated 55,131 pounds of food.

David's perseverance at such a young age has been an inspiration for those hoping to make an impact on society in spite of government. To David, "perseverance" has meant never giving up. Not once, he said, during this whole experience did he think about failing.

Unfortunately, though, this young boy has had to persevere over more than just a bureaucracy. Others his age did not quite appreciate his good deeds and the attention he was gaining as a result of them. David was ridiculed by many of his peers because what he did wasn't "cool." He had to overcome teasing *and* being roughed up. He was called "charity boy" and was chased by a group of boys who knocked his trumpet from his bike while shouting anti-Semitic slurs at him. The teasing and name calling have made David even more determined.

In his own life, David's biggest influence has been his

parents, especially his caring mother, who "keeps me straight," he says. David has seen his parents' involvement in their temple and how they have effected change. These actions were the motivating factor for his food donation program. He credits his religion and temple, which have taught him the importance of being a responsible citizen. In addition, one of his school teachers, Lucy Bertrand, has had a tremendous impact on him. According to David, she had not only taught him how to critically think through problems, but she also provided unconditional support, often attending many of David's out of school extracurricular activities. She taught him how to believe in his own abilities.

Because of his significant and permanent contributions to his community, David has received both local and national recognition. He was invited to address Harvest U.S.A.'s national convention in Kentucky in March 1995, where he shared the spotlight with former Vice President Dan Quayle. In typical teenager fashion, he gushes at the fact that he sat next to Miss America during a dinner and received a personal note from her. But this notoriety has not deterred him. It is David's continuing influence in leading others to work on behalf of the hungry that has truly made him a profile in character. Since seeing through the implementation of his program, he has continued to convince restaurant owners and event organizers to donate their unserved food to shelters. At his own bar mitzvah, he asked guests to bring food instead of gifts. As a result, more than five hundred pounds of food were donated to Tampa Bay Harvest. David was most touched by a letter he received from his old baby-sitter, Mindy, who was unable to attend the celebration because she was away at college. Mindy could not afford to buy him a present because she was struggling to pay for her own education. So her gift to David was time donated in his honor to a shelter near her campus. David will never forget that gift.

This winter, David, now fourteen, will venture north to Tallahassee to lobby the Florida State legislature and secretary of education for passage of a resolution he helped draft that would expand his leftover lunch program statewide. David will once again go up against Goliath with the same determination and will to persevere. In doing so he will remember and scoff at one of his favorite lines from a movie, *The Fugitive*, spoken by actor Tommy Lee Jones—"Don't mess with the big dogs because the big dogs are always right." David Levitt knows better.

# Delwyn Collins: Earning His Angel Wings

## *Tampa, Florida*

*There are no limits to what a man can do as long as he does not care who gets the credit. People who truly demonstrate character and virtue are those who do not seek personal fame or glory; rather, they act out of a common sense of good. For years, a man in Tampa has been quietly practicing the virtue of compassion by anonymously providing holiday joy to foster children and single mothers. His recent discovery provides a lesson to us all about the true meaning of Christmas.*

He is a quiet, unassuming man working in a corner of the kitchen at Tampa General Hospital. Dressed in green hospital smocks and donning thick-lensed glasses to correct his almost blind vision, he can be found either swishing a mop around the floor or delivering food trays. Handicapped since childhood with a learning disability, he earns about six dollars an hour at a job he has held for seven years. He volunteers to work holidays and starts wearing a Santa hat at Thanksgiving time. His name is Delwyn Collins.

In 1992, Delwyn Collins noticed something unusual at the hospital. "They put a regular Christmas tree up in the middle of the dining area," said Collins. "They had it all lit up and decorated, there was a big star on top, and there were about five hundred names of kids dangling from different limbs. You just couldn't miss all those names with their ages listed on the back."

It was the first year Tampa General had put up an angel tree, sponsored by a local foster children's program. The names of hundreds of underprivileged children were scrawled on paper angel ornaments. The ornaments hung on the tree waiting for some hospital employee or patient to remove them and assume responsibility for delivering a toy for that particular child to the hospital. That year, Delwyn Collins pulled twenty ornaments from the tree.

The following year he took more ornaments. By Christmas of 1994, Collins was taking thirty-seven ornaments from the tree. For years Collins's work was done anonymously. He would save up all year-round, working hard at his low-paying job just to earn enough money for the toys. Most years he did not have enough money, so he would do odd jobs for the neighbors near his south Tampa apartment. He would then pull the ornaments off the tree, buy the toys and deliver them to the hospital. He would buy the batteries too since "you want to be sure that when they wake up Christmas morning, they have batteries to make the toys work," says Collins. But nobody knew.

Collins does not drive a car, so he had problems transporting the toys he bought to the hospital. Before people took notice, he would just load the toys on his bicycle—in his basket or tying them to whatever part of the bicycle he could—and pedal to work along Bayshore Boulevard. Sometimes, he would put them in a wagon and pull that along. One year, his friend Ruddy McCarter picked him up in his truck. The toys nearly filled the truck. Trying to get all these toys to the hospital finally led to the discovery of this secret Santa Claus.

In early December 1994, Collins was pulling his wagon through the hospital when he was stopped by one of the hospital's supervisors. The supervisor asked Collins if the hospital was already starting to deliver the toys to the children *from* the angel tree. Collins responded that all the toys were from him and that he was bringing them *to* the angel tree for the children. Soon the world would come to share in the character and compassion that moves Delwyn Collins. "I didn't realize it would touch a lot of people," Delwyn said.

Collins had to adjust to all the attention. The local and national media came calling as well as the civic leaders of Tampa, who awarded him the Hillsborough County Moral Courage Award in 1995. Numerous public officials with tremendous name recognition and large constituencies had been nominated, but this humble kitchen worker beat them all out. Even his actual nomination for this award came about because of Collins's act of selflessness. The person who nominated Collins was a dental surgeon who saw a newspaper article on the angel tree. Recognizing Collins in the article as a patient of hers, she checked his record and noticed that he had not made an appointment for surgery he needed. Collins told the dentist's office manager that he chose not to have it done so he could continue saving up money for the children.

For most of his life, Collins has been inspired by a simple but powerful goodness inside that drives him to help. He grew up poor in Texas and his father, who was a railroad engineer, died when Collins was only ten years old. He was raised by his mother, Dorothy, who had to work two jobs just to keep her four children fed and clothed. It was this experience that gave him a special affinity to the plight of single mothers and their children. "I like helping single mothers and kids and I see what the kids have gone through in this day and age. We focus on the other countries, but we do not focus on our problems with our kids.... Parents are killed or on drugs, and these kids really do not have a home to go to." Last Thanksgiving the hospital passed out turkeys to all the employees. Collins gave his turkey away to a family in need. He is also sponsoring two single mothers whom he helps out during the holidays.

Collins has used his good character to overcome a lot. Throughout most of his childhood, he attended special education schools and participated in the Special Olympics. He says, "It has been hard to deal with the disabilities." He recalls being twenty-one years old and not knowing how to read, not knowing how to make out the words on an application that would determine if he was eligible for Social Security. Delwyn Collins has not let his learning disability deter him from living a productive life and helping others. Today, Collins lives by himself with no children of his own, but his mother lives nearby.

Because of all the attention attracted by Collins and the angel tree, people have been sending in contributions to help, and the hospital has formed a foundation to collect the funds in his name. Collins gathered 153 toys this year, including 8 bicycles, with the money that had been collected. But this additional help has not meant his job is any easier. He is still determined to buy with his own money all the toys for the 40 angels he pulled off the tree. Collins says he was very busy in the fall, spending many a late night wrapping the toys and placing ribbons around the packages.

Delwyn Collins is living proof that random, simple acts of kindness can make a difference. He believes that a world full of persons of good character is a world full of people "who like doing things for others and ask for nothing in return and couldn't care less about what they were getting back." For the children of Tampa in need who will receive gifts from Delwyn Collins this year, they may never know it but they have been touched by the best kind of character, a person whose only wish is to place "happiness in their hearts."

# Janet Campbell Gray: Laying "Can't" to Rest

*Lake Helen, Florida*

> A teacher who can arouse a feeling for one single good
> action ... accomplishes more than he who fills our
> memory with rows on rows of natural objects, classified
> with name and form.
>
> —*Johann Wolfgang von Goethe*
> Elective Affinities, *Book II, Chapter 7*

*Teachers and schools often are part of that local network of
"little platoons" that instill character in our children.
Teachers oversee our kids about seven hours out of each day,
often spending more time with our children on a daily basis
than we are able to as parents. Many of us have had a
favorite teacher whom we can look back on with fondness.
For many students in Lake Helen, Janet Campbell Gray is
already that teacher. Her passion for teaching and love of
children are no small reflection of her own perseverance in
overcoming childhood problems and dropping out of school.*

There is a fifth-grade class at Lake Helen Elementary
School like no other. Debussy's classical composition
*Claire de Lune* plays softly in the background of this
cozy room as Mattie Kay, a pet pig, wanders from student to student. Blue-and-red-checkered curtains hang
from the wall, giving this classroom a very homey feel.
In one corner of the room sits an antique bathtub filled
with pillows, which serves as a place for students to
"soak up their problems" or "scrub up on mathematics." As unusual as this scholastic setting sounds, you
know right away that there is a lot of love and learning
going on in this classroom. The inspirational teacher

behind this classroom is Janet Campbell Gray, a forty-six-year-old instructor who as a teenager quit school herself but somehow managed to raise a family, return to school to receive her teaching degree and in just six years become Volusia County's Teacher of the Year for 1994–1995.

Her uplifting story is a testament to her love of education, her faith, her determination and her own creative energy. But life was not always a proverbial bowl of cherries for Gray. Her own childhood years were the complete antithesis of everything she represents today. Gray now shares with her students the gifts she developed only after years of pain.

Gray grew up in a rural part of West Virginia so desolate that there was literally no running water. She tells of the poverty she experienced living in one of the poorest states in the nation. Raised by a father who was an alcoholic and frequently unemployed, her family oftentimes could not pay the rent. As a result, they would abandon their home in the middle of the night, leaving many of their personal belongings behind, and all of the friendships she would have to develop over and over again. (As a small child, Gray attended at least six different elementary schools in West Virginia, Kentucky, South Carolina and Florida.) She remembers one particular midnight move when after driving for a while, her father stopped the car and for no apparent reason made her leave behind her ten-year-old dog, Tippy, whom she had raised from a puppy. She recalls her hysterical sobs as she begged her father to at least take the dog back to their old home. She also remembers her mother trying to make the best of an awful situation by telling her, "Janet, it will be all right.

I saw a big white house back there with children playing in the yard. I know Tippy will be happy there. Don't worry."

But Gray knew there was no white house and no children playing in the yard, only a mother's efforts to help ease the pain of yet another erratic and often traumatic decision made by Gray's father. Her father continued drinking, and he tried to commit suicide, many times in Gray's presence. Often, she would have to take him to the hospital. She missed a lot of school as a result of her father's problems and because she had to care for the younger children while her mother worked day and night. When Gray was in the eighth grade, her family moved to St. Augustine. In one of her classes, a teacher told her, "Of course you don't understand the work. You are never here. Why don't you just quit?" So she did.

At age eighteen, she received a call to come to the hospital. After so many previously failed suicide attempts, she expected to find her father alive and recovering. But this time he had succeeded. Gray turned the page in her life.

Two years later, she married John, who became the stabilizing force that she needed in her life after so much trauma and tragedy. Together, they had two children and moved to Lake Helen. Her rough and transient background had taught her that a stable community was important. So during her kids' childhood years, Gray became involved in Brownies, Girl Scouts, Cub Scouts, Little League and taught Sunday school. She tutored and volunteered for the Right to Read program and Meals on Wheels. When her older child entered elementary school, Gray vowed that her own children's schooling would be dramatically different from her own. If it was up to Gray, her children would never suffer the humiliation she had experienced as a student. She volunteered in her son's class as a way of making sure he was performing well, and in 1980, she was hired as a teacher's assistant to Alzada Fowler. Fowler was an inspiration to Gray. She was patient, caring and understanding. After serving as a mentor for Gray for six years, Fowler said one day, "Why don't you get up off your good intentions and get a class of your own?" Only Gray's incomplete education stood in the way. She was terrified of having to go back to school with only an eighth-grade education. However, at the age of thirty-five, Gray proudly received her high school diploma and by 1990, she had graduated with honors in elementary education from the University of Central Florida.

Gray juggled family, school and church responsibilities in her rekindled school years. In her Sunday school classes during those years she began implementing such innovative ways to tell stories from the Bible that her enrollment increased from six students to thirty-six students in just three months.

In her first year as a teacher, at the elementary school where it all began, Gray received the Sallie Mae Beginning Teacher of the Year Award for her ability to inspire and make students feel special. She believes this is the result of a special gift she acquired in her childhood. "I know what it is to feel talented and then not be able to use those talents," she says. The students in this relatively poor and rural part of the state feel cared for and are inspired by her love. She teaches them to rise above adversity. As part of her relationships with the kids, Gray has an arrangement with a local florist to deliver a flower to each student on his or her birthday. She also takes that student out for breakfast on the following Saturday. Her first class of the year always begins with a simple funeral service, where they lay the word "can't" to rest under an old oak tree. With "can't" out of the way, her students are free to shoot for the stars. Everyone becomes an involved, productive member of her class.

Gray literally believes in a hands-on approach to education: She believes children can love learning more if they can touch. Her room is filled with stuffed and live animals and computers. Students read books and then answer questions on the computer. On special occasions, there are tea parties and elegant meals served on Gray's own silver and crystal from home. Most of her students show up early and do not want to leave after class. Teachers and interns from all over come to observe Gray in action. They travel to see firsthand some of Gray's innovative economic projects. For example, one of her classes went into a partnership with a Georgia peanut farmer and split the profits. Another of her classes, with the support of thirty-three local businesses, raised a steer and a heifer, winning blue ribbons at the 1995 county fair.

At the end of the 1995–1996 school year, the ninety-year-old Lake Helen Elementary School closes its doors forever. Janet Campbell Gray moves to a new school where she will not miss a beat. Already, she is planning an agriscience class for children in kindergarten through the fifth grade, and she has written Honda Corporation for a grant. Her proposed classroom will include five acres devoted to raising animals, farming and science.

Looking at many of her students, Gray worries about our culture and the dysfunctional families that are present even in her small town. She sees many young children raising themselves because both parents work. She believes we must restore godly principles in society and lessen our reliance on government. Gray is a firm believer that parents and teachers should be able to discipline children without Health and Rehabilitative Services or any other agency coming down on them after seeing only part of the problem.

But most important, Janet Campbell Gray believes that parents, grandparents and members of the community should become more involved in the schools, as she did at Lake Helen Elementary. She believes that community involvement will assist in the chronic funding shortfall education faces in Florida. Gray writes, "A community is like a body with each part working to enhance the other. When one part is missing, the body is no longer whole. Quality education requires everyone working together."

As a final thought, she states, "A love for learning must radiate from the teacher in order for a love of learning to radiate from the student. Teaching comes from deep within. A concerned, caring teacher is constantly under self-evaluation and strives to improve with each day. A teacher is not hired from 8:00 A.M. to 2:00 P.M., but from her first day as a teacher until retirement. Teaching never ends. It follows you to the grocery store. It becomes your every thought and is the last thought on your mind as you turn in for the night."

Gray knows the key to success in young peoples' lives: Believe in them, value them, love them, give them attention, cheer them on and guide them to their dreams. How fortunate are the thousands of future students in Lake Helen who will be touched by the passionate teaching of Janet Campbell Gray.

# Darrel Teel: Finding Honesty in a Field of Dreams

## *Orlando, Florida*

*In a world full of extramarital affairs, students who cheat on exams, Miss America contestants who pad their résumés and, of course, say-anything politicians, what role does the virtue of honesty play in our society? Honesty is about the truth—being truthful with others and truthful with ourselves. Just as with the other virtues, honesty is a necessary component of character. But as Irish bishop and philosopher George Berkeley once said, "Truth is the cry of all, but the game of few." The following story is about an unlikely one of those few.*

Today, sixty-two-year-old Darrel Teel lives and works out west in Sulphur Springs, Texas. He has a steady job as a plumber's assistant, his own apartment and just recently he bought a truck, which he uses for work. On Sundays, if he is not working, Teel likes to go to church with his sister. It all sounds very normal. But there was a time in Darrel Teel's life when things were not so well ordered.

In 1991, Teel was a drifter. He had hitchhiked from the Midwest all the way to Florida and found himself in the Orlando area. Once in Orlando, he spent his days working in a labor pool for pocket change. At night, he spent his earnings getting drunk and sleeping under a piece of carpet in the woods. He lived life day to day, never thinking too far ahead, just trying to survive another day in the dangerous world of the homeless.

His luck was about to change for the better. Early one February morning, somewhere off South Orange Blossom Trail, Teel was walking through an empty lot behind a local bar on his way to the labor pool. He was shuffling through trash searching for cigarette butts to smoke. Teel had just spent his last dollar on a beer and had only nine cents left in his pocket when he spied what appeared to be a heap of garbage. He dug his hand into the pile and pulled out a stuffed envelope. Looking down, he saw that there were two more stuffed envelopes just like the first. To his surprise, when he opened the envelopes, all three contained several hundred one-hundred-dollar bills—more money in one place than Teel had ever seen.

"I didn't count the money right there, but I knew it was a lot," says Teel in a deep Texas drawl. "The first thing I thought was that I was going to get me a haircut and a suit so I could go back to Texas to see my grandson." However, Teel did not go directly to the barber or department store with his newly found wealth. Instead, he walked around the block, realizing the great moral dilemma with which he was faced. It seemed as if everyone was staring at him and he began to feel what he described as a great weight upon him. He thought to himself for a bit. Teel asked, "What would my grandson think if they caught me as a thief?" The decision was made.

Teel called 911 from a pay phone, but no one answered. So he walked a mile to the nearest jailhouse with nearly $30,000 in his coat pocket. When he reached the jailhouse, he rang the security bell several times before a clerk finally opened the door. Hoping to lift the great weight, he gave the $29,200 to one of the officers. Before he knew it, however, he was surrounded by several other officers, who began questioning him about the money. Skeptical, the officers asked him to tell his story over and over again, letting Teel know he was in a bunch of trouble. Hoping to buttress his story, he led them to where he had found the small fortune. The officers soon found information that led to the identity of the woman who had lost the money. It belonged to a woman who distrusted banks and carried her life savings around with her wherever she went. On this particular shopping trip, she had lost her money. The woman rewarded Teel for his honesty by giving him $200, and the drifter went back to his daily routine.

Teel's unbelievable story was not unlike that of the downtrodden George Bailey in the classic Frank Capra film *It's a Wonderful Life*. The community soon rallied around him for his Jimmy Stewart-like honesty. By the next morning, he was a celebrity although he did not know it. Sergeant Richard Henderson, the officer to whom Teel had turned over the money, searched for him all morning long. He finally found him drinking with another labor pool worker. Overnight, local businesses that had heard about Teel's story made job offers and other donations. The press was also in search of "the man who turned in more money than he had ever made in his entire life." Everybody wanted to know why this fellow down on his luck would turn in all this money. Teel told reporters, "I thought God would punish me for taking something that wasn't mine."

In the wake of the media attention, much of it national, Teel was given a job in Orlando at Builder's Square, helping to load merchandise for customers. He thought his $4.50 an hour job was "really living." Local businesses and the community set him up in a furnished duplex apartment, and Teel was adopted by Brownie troop #174. At a surprise ceremony in the Casselberry Elementary School cafeteria, Teel was met by hugs from the Brownie troop. They had saved up money to buy him a television set for his new apartment. He sat with the girls and read the cards they had made for him. "Did you ever see so much love?" he asked the troop leader. Many of the Brownies found a moral hero in Darrel Teel. The seven-year-olds said that Teel deserved the gift because he was trustworthy and honest. But Teel could not understand what all the fuss was about. He told reporters that he did not want to be rewarded for his honest deed. All he wanted was self-respect.

Years later, Teel credits his parents and the church for the way things turned out in Orlando. Teel was born the oldest of ten children in a labor camp in Kansas. At age twelve, he worked side by side with his father in the cotton fields and onion patches of McKinney, a farming community north of Dallas. Most of the time his parents were sick and could not work, so Teel had to pick up the slack. "I often had to watch the kids and work because of my parents' health," he told us. Despite these difficult times, Teel describes his childhood as the happiest time of his life. He fondly remembers going to the Baptist church with his mother every Sunday. He also remembers the closeness of his parents. "My parents were always together." He never saw them apart until his mother passed away at the age of fifty-two. "She is the best person I ever knew."

Teel believes he learned the importance of many virtues, including honesty, through his father. He remembers being disciplined by his father for having stolen a bicycle from a neighbor. Teel, in turn, was able to pass this lesson in honesty down to his own children when he found a stolen bicycle in his son's possession. "I made him return it to the neighbor and tell her that he would work to make up for it. So she made him mow her lawn. He mowed it once and she paid him for it."

After nine years of marriage and three children, Teel divorced the woman he had met in Oklahoma, an event that led to his transient lifestyle. He eventually made his way to Florida. Yet he always longed to return to Texas to see his children and grandchildren. That is why after all the attention and warmth he received from the Orlando community, he still wanted to be back with his family. Sergeant Henderson, who had helped Teel adjust to all the attention, knew that Teel was unhappy. Says Henderson, "He really didn't want to be in the situation he was in, but he had been in that environment for so long that he didn't know how to get out." So after working at Builder's Square for three months, Darrel Teel packed up his few belongings and moved back to Texas.

Even today, Teel is uncomfortable with his role as a model of honesty for young people. Yet he strongly believes there are many problems in society that are a result of the breakdown of the family. According to Teel, "People aren't close enough to their kids. They don't go to ball games and things like that. They just sit at home and watch TV. They should go fishin' together and get to know each other." The man who knows what it is like to be without a home and a family knows. "Family is important. If they don't keep up with each other, then they're missing their whole lives, and they don't have anything to live for."

Reflecting on his past, Darrel Teel realizes that his own life has not been picture perfect. However, he believes he has always aimed to do what is right by himself and by God. The moral of the Darrel Teel story as he describes it is a simple one: "I believe in prayer ... anywhere. I'm just an average person, but I say you gotta try to improve yourself." To young people, he says, "Be yourself. Use common sense, try hard and join sports teams or clubs because you learn to work hard and get along with others. That is important."

Teel's single honest act is only a small part of the larger character of the man. It is a personal character built by the lessons of growing up in a strong and stable family—a family that taught him the difference between right and wrong and the virtue of honesty. It is a virtue that has been powerful enough to bring him back to his family.

# Thomas LeRoy Collins: Moral Leadership for a State

## Tallahassee, Florida

> Once to every man and nation
> Comes the moment to decide,
> In the strife of truth with falsehood,
> For the Good or Evil side.
> —*Governor Collins at his inaugural quoting a hymn*
> *by abolitionist James Russell Lowell*[3]

*Contrary to conventional wisdom, men and women of character can be found among those who hold public office or who work for the government. In this regard, Thomas LeRoy Collins stands out. As governor and in other positions of state and national importance, he provided the necessary moral leadership at a time when Florida was struggling between continuing as a relic of the old South or emerging as the leader of the new South. Collins is also our only historical profile in character, appearing in his capacity as perhaps the most influential public person in our state's history. Upon his death in 1991, the Florida legislature passed a resolution honoring LeRoy Collins as "Floridian of the Century." This is the story of a good man who was forced to deal with one of the great moral issues of our time. Prudence and integrity were the virtues he employed.*

At a time roughly ninety years before LeRoy Collins would become the governor of the State of Florida, another tall, gallant, gentle man, this one from the prairies of Illinois, was trying to convince a nation that it was time to abide by common notions of morality, that all men should be free and equal and that slavery was an abomination of our every sense of goodness. As a candidate for office, he had preached this for years. As president, Abraham Lincoln recognized the difficult task ahead. There was much change that needed to occur and Lincoln had to present his moral position in terms acceptable to the general masses. This would require prudence and respect for the limits of the president's constitutional powers. His main priority at the time was trying to win a war that would preserve the Union.

And so the Emancipation Proclamation was born. It was a military order issued by the commander in chief in the midst of a war. But it did not demand equal political or civil rights for all blacks. It merely read that slaves would be free in those states that were still in rebellion come January 1, 1863. For areas that were no longer in rebellion, slavery would continue. Lincoln used this military pretext within his constitutional powers to carry out what is now widely regarded as a moral act as significant as the Declaration of Independence.

Early on and into the twilight of his two terms as governor of Florida in the 1950s and 1960s, the stately yet folksy LeRoy Collins had to convince Floridians that our state was not like the rest of the South and that Florida had to be a leader when it came to recognizing the inevitability of equal political and civil rights for blacks. At this time in our state's history, his was a message as sensitive as Lincoln's. Governors all over the South, such as Orville Faubus of Arkansas and George Wallace of Alabama (he of "Segregation now! Segregation tomorrow! Segregation forever!" fame), were riding the wave of popular support for segregation. So Collins would have to show the same leadership and self-discipline as Lincoln in trying to sway Florida to do what was right.

LeRoy Collins was born and raised in Tallahassee in the early 1900s, the son of a grocer. His family life was one touched by piety and the church, a high regard for education, involvement in the community and hard work. Collins spent many a summer working on his grandfather's farm north of Tallahassee. There was no alcohol or vulgar language in the Collins family and misbehavior was punished. Children in the Collins household were taught to treat blacks politely and not to use their presumed superior status as whites to foster abuse. LeRoy Collins was popular growing up. He obtained a law degree and practiced for a number of years before being elected to the Florida House of Representatives. After six years there, he moved on to the Florida Senate, where he served until 1944. In 1946, after a stint in the military and reelection, he resumed his old position in the Florida State Senate, a position Collins kept until deciding to run for governor.

By 1955, Collins found himself, as a governor, in the throes of the great moral crisis of this century. In May of 1954, in an election to fill the governorship left vacant by the untimely death of Dan McCarty, LeRoy Collins had beat out Charley Johns for the Democratic nomination, guaranteeing him a win in November. To accomplish what was right, Collins had to work within the confines of the spirit of the times. The U.S. Supreme Court had just handed down two very unpopular decisions in *Brown* v. *Board of Education* and a second *Brown* decision, which together mandated public school desegregation and gave full authority to unelected federal judges to carry out the task. Polls at this time in Florida showed that better than 80 percent of the population opposed federally mandated desegregation. Massive segregation movements began to pop up around the South. A politician's stand on race became a litmus test for most white voters. Legislatures passed laws shoring up segregation. Black sit-ins and boycotts ensued.

At first, LeRoy Collins did not fervently advocate the equal rights espoused in these court decisions. During his first term as governor, Collins instead adopted a "gradualist" position. He did not denounce desegregation as other governors in the South were doing, but he implored federal courts to make the changes slowly to give whites time to become accustomed to change and to prevent violent confrontations. He would not make extreme statements that favored either side of the debate. This infuriated many blacks and whites alike. Years later, in 1981, he addressed a predominantly black audience at Florida A&M University and explained his early position. Collins said,

> I do not want to appear defensive as to my own efforts, but I do ask your understanding of the conditions which influenced some of the things I said and did in response to my duty as I then saw it…. But I hope historians will understand the broad responsibility I had to lead a reform program in Florida which required the support of the majority of the people. I hope also that I will be judged as having perceived and given some support to eternal values.[4]

Collins recognized that to come out totally in favor of desegregation would give rise to a backlash of segregationist sentiments and probably lead to the installation of a segregationist governor in 1956. He had to seek moderation.

After his first term as governor, LeRoy Collins faced reelection and a challenge from a militant segregationist, Sumter Lowry. Lowry favored a doctrine historically popular in the South known as interposition. This doctrine was the same as the old doctrine of nullification employed by John C. Calhoun of South Carolina in the late 1820s in which a state could nullify a federal law or decision of the Supreme Court, as the segregationists would have it. Collins fervently opposed interposition.

Like Lincoln, he campaigned for prudence on the

race issue. Whereas Lincoln used military necessity as a pretext for change, Collins astutely used economic necessity for change. He focused on economic progress and reapportionment. He told voters, "Nothing will turn ... investors away quicker than the prospect of finding here communities hopped up by demagoguery and seething under the tension and turmoil of race hatred."[5] The strategy worked as voters recognized Florida's economic position was more key to its future than its racial position. Collins was reelected decisively.

Unable by law to run for election a third time, Collins was able to spread his wings in his second term and show more boldness with his moral conscience on the race issue. His second inaugural address set the tone:

> We can find wise solutions if the white citizens will face up to the fact that the Negro does not now have equal opportunities, that he is morally and legally entitled to progress more rapidly, and that a full good-faith effort should be made forthwith to help him move forward in the improvement of all his standards.... God forbid that it shall ever be said of our administration, "They did not have the vision to see," or seeing, "They did not have the will to try."... Ours is the generation in which great decisions can no longer be passed to the next. We have a State to build—a South to save—a nation to convince—and a God to serve.[6]

Early into that second term, Collins urged legislators not to act on a resolution for interposition, one that Collins had no power to veto. Unfortunately, in the regular legislative session of 1957, a resolution was passed. Collins could no longer stay silent. On the measure itself, he penned a bold statement asserting his legacy as a man of principle. He denounced interposition as "an evil thing, whipped up by the demagogues and carried on the hot and erratic winds of passion, prejudice, and hysteria.... I want it known that I did my best to avert this blot. If I am judged wrong, then here in my own handwriting and over my signature is the proof of guilt to support my conviction."[7]

LeRoy Collins did all he could throughout his second term to convince Florida not to fall victim to the segregationists' siren song. In 1957, he vetoed a bill that would have given school boards the authority to shut down schools rather than admit black schoolchildren. In both the Tallahassee bus boycott of 1957 and the lunch-counter sit-ins and demonstrations of early 1960, Collins did all he could to prevent violence and continued to appeal to the people on moral grounds. This made Collins enormously popular outside the South, but a traitor of sorts among many in his own state and among other southerners. Nevertheless, it was the perception of Florida to the rest of the nation that was critical. People outside Florida recognized that Florida was different from the other southern states. It was more tempered and progressive than its neighbors. It was also a state led by a man of vision, conviction and courage. In the long run, our state would come to benefit from Collins's leadership, not so much for what he did to tear down the walls of racial injustice but for his efforts to prevent our state from falling down a slippery slope that haunted other southern states for years. Although Floridians did not know it at the time, Collins was paving the way to make Florida one of the most influential states in the Union.

In perhaps his last true act of moral courage and leadership as governor of Florida, LeRoy Collins decided in 1960 to give a televised statewide address that would provide his final and definitive statement on the race issue. The address was designed to comment on the lunch-counter sit-ins that were taking place all around the state. The station crew in Jacksonville was friendly to Collins and excited as air time approached. At 5:30 P.M., Collins began his statement. He told Florida, "As long as I am in this office, I will say what I think is right. I will not have on my conscience a feeling that at any time the people needed my help, I ducked or dodged or looked the other way in order to follow the easy course." He continued, "I think the people of this state expect their governor to have convictions, and I think the people of this state, when their governor has convictions about a matter, expect him to express those convictions directly to them." He explained that although business owners had a legal right to refuse service to blacks at a lunch counter, he did not believe they had a moral right. Collins explained that businessmen in this position were not taking a "Christian point of view" and that the ideal that all men are created equal should be a reality and not an "illusory distant goal."

According to one biographer, Collins had sealed his fate in Florida on that night. After that speech, the station crew sat stunned and silenced. Their friendliness disappeared as Collins looked out at their blank stares. He left the television studio without a word being spoken. Collins never won elective office in Florida again.

In the ensuing years, LeRoy Collins became more prominent as a national figure than as a state figure. He chaired the 1960 Democratic National Convention and years later accepted Lyndon B. Johnson's offer to head the Community Relations Service, which was created to oversee peaceful desegregation. It was in this position that Collins found himself with Dr. Martin Luther King, Jr., at the Edmund Pettis Bridge in Selma, Alabama, in 1965. Collins was there to mediate but photographs capturing the moment appeared to show Collins marching with King's group. It was a picture that would reappear in his last unsuccessful run for public office— the U.S. Senate in 1968.

LeRoy Collins's lasting legacy in Florida will be the conviction and foresight he had to move Florida into a new progressive era. As we shift to another era being defined as this book is being read, Floridians know that the inevitable change that comes with it is turbulent and traumatic. By drawing on the moral principles that guided his life, LeRoy Collins was like a steady beacon of character that showed Floridians the way through the storm, moving us into an era of unprecedented growth and opportunity. It could not have been done by sheer political skills alone. Let us hope that our leaders use the same timeless principles to show us the way to the next era of opportunity.

# Dorothy Perry:
# A Mother's Dream

## Miami, Florida

*Dorothy Perry knows how important it is to be loved by a family. So she worries about the children in the public housing projects who are growing up in broken households or with parents who are less than responsible. Over the years, this compassion has swelled into a full-time avocation as Dorothy ("Mizz Dot") Perry now finds herself serving as a mother to dozens of children in need of the stability of a family. She loves them all as if they were her own and in the process is helping to save lives. Perry is a profile in love who teaches the virtue of responsibility.*

To first-time visitors, the buildings and streets of the James E. Scott housing project look like something out of a bad dream: drab, prefabricated apartments; trash in the yards; children wandering aimlessly in the streets; dogs leashed with rope or chain. The aura of poverty hovers like a thick blanket of humidity on a summer day in South Florida.

But something is different about 2167 Northwest 69th Terrace. The back door is open to the parking lot. The rich aroma of a greasy breakfast—eggs, bacon, grits, all the trimmings—wafts out the door. There is singing, laughing, talking. Children's voices. And the voice that can be heard above them all is that of Dorothy Perry.

Twenty years ago, Dorothy Perry moved here with three boys and two girls of her own. Today, she is surrogate mother to more that thirty-five children ranging in age from one to twenty-one. These are "her kids." They are the children of Liberty City—children who had little hope until they met "Mizz Dot."

They came from broken homes, homes where parents were strung out on crack or alcohol, where parents worked three and four jobs and had no energy left to care for the children when and if they came home. Dorothy Perry remembers moving into 2167 and having to step over children in her own doorway just to get inside. She remembers the foul language and the fights breaking out hourly. But Mizz Dott refused to accept it.

Thus began Youths Progressing in Public Housing, a nonprofit program whose mission is to provide a stable home atmosphere for children who have no stability in their lives. Youths Progressing serves as a temporary safe haven for abused and displaced children. But equally important, it serves as a role model that promotes the development of leadership and teaches inner city children they can do something positive and handle responsibilities. In short, Perry teaches children to wipe out hopelessness and to embrace self-help.

Perry's one-woman show is a school about life that may be as good as or better than anything her kids will get in the classroom. It's also a reminder of the power of individuals. Whether it's home economics and coupon clipping, Bible class and singing or weekly "ambition rap" sessions, Perry keeps her kids busy and doesn't hesitate to discipline them along the way.

"Many of the parents of my kids were raised without values in the home," Perry says. "And when that happens, you don't pass any on to your children.

"When the kids arrive in my house for the first time, we have a rap session, and I let them know the rules: respecting yourself, respecting others and other people's property. Become a role model, mind your manners, stay away from trouble. Your walk, talk and code of dress will be different here. I don't sugar-coat it. It won't be easy, I tell them. But if you make up your mind to do the right thing, you have to stick to it," says Perry.

Some kids resist. They tell Perry, "You can't tell me what to do. You're not my mom." "And I say, 'That's right. You can do whatever you want in your mom's house. What you do in my house is another story. I represent your mom here.'"

Born in 1941, Perry was sent at age five to live with her grandmother in Georgia when her parents separated. Perry's grandmother Sweetie Gross, the daughter of slaves, had a strong spiritual background and was a pillar of strength for the young Perry.

"I knew that I was growing up in a family atmosphere because of her. Everybody pitched in to help raise someone else's child. My aunt's children were always there. And I know that what I'm doing today is simply what I grew up with because of her."

Perry and her husband separated when their children were young. It was then that Perry made a promise to her children. "They might lack many things, but they would never lack their mother's love. I would always be there," she says.

Honored by everyone from President Ronald Reagan to *Washington Post* columnist William Raspberry, Perry maintains an unusually low profile—by choice. "In a day and age where everybody is looking for recognition, my mom could care less," says Lynnette Dopson, Perry's youngest daughter and treasurer of Youths Progressing.

Perry has work to do. "In order to do the work, I can't be high-minded," Perry says. "The Bible says we have to be humble, and I know I'm a servant of God and other people before myself."

"I bring people from all over the nation to Dade County to see Ms. Dorothy Perry," says Robert L. Woodson, Sr., president of a Washington, D.C.-based self-help organization called the National Center for Neighborhood Enterprise.

"I call her the Mother Teresa of public housing," Woodson adds. "That's how institutions should be built, not raising money to bring in social workers and others from the outside with degrees. Love is what cures people."

Youths Progressing is literally a nonprofit organization. Perry provides meals, clothes and recreational activities fueled with the contributions of small private donations and the money she personally saves and can scrape together. Volunteer legal services filed the paperwork to incorporate Perry's program. They told her there was no need to file for charity status because no one would ever put money into her program. So Perry's daughter filed the Internal Revenue Service application. Since then, it hasn't been easy. Several times the government has attempted to evict her because of space and occupancy rules, which restrict programs like Perry's from operating in individual public housing units. But she doesn't think about the money.

"There have been so many stumbling blocks. If it wasn't for my faith in God, I would have given up. But I can't take time to worry about where the money will come from because if I did, I wouldn't get any work done."

Has Perry made a difference? Eighteen-year-old Quintin Varnedoe came to live with her at age seven after his mother died. "It's been great. I've learned a lot, and she's kept me out of trouble. My brothers were in gangs, telling me to sell drugs and rob to get money, but Mizz Dot was keeping me busy." Quintin will soon leave for South Carolina to enlist in the Marine Corps.

"I think this program saved my life." That's how James Holley, twenty, describes Dorothy Perry's work. "My mother was having problems with drugs, and the state was talking about taking me from her. I didn't have anywhere to go, so I just came and talked to Mizz Dot. Without her, I don't know where I would be right now.... She just keeps on giving me chances." Now Holley is working toward receiving his general equivalency diploma.

"I have a dream," Perry says, "that God tells me to get on an airplane and land in the middle of a big green field. And all the poor children of the world will be there. And I'll put them in the plane and take them home with me and love them."

Perry has another dream: purchasing a home with a garden outside of the Scott housing project where she can take care of her children in a better environment.

"When you come here," Perry tells the children, "we practice love hugs. When you come here, you become part of a family. This is a gang where there is no violence—only love and respect."

# Irving Graifman: The Will to Survive

## *Tamarac, Florida*

*The steady migration of elderly people to Florida seeking a comfortable retirement has also brought with it people of wisdom and experience who are willing to teach our children about virtue. It is a precious resource we must rely upon in this era of cultural decline. Perhaps no group is as qualified to discuss character with our children as are the many Holocaust survivors who have settled in South Florida. Their tales of fortitude, courage and faith should be passed down for generations to come. One group, the Holocaust Survivors of South Florida, is doing just that. They are talking to our schoolchildren, sharing their pain so that history will never again repeat itself. There were many survivors who could have been profiled in these pages as all their stories are emotionally compelling. We selected Irving Graifman, the president of the Holocaust Survivors of South Florida.*

Irving Graifman grew up in a large family in Poland. Besides his mother and father, he lived with four brothers, three sisters and an orphaned cousin whom his parents were raising. Today, at the age of seventy-two, there is only Graifman and a brother, Alex, who is four years older. They both live in Tamarac. Sunday, November 27, 1995, marked a joyous occasion in Graifman's life: He and his wife, Ruth, celebrated their fiftieth wedding anniversary among one hundred friends and family members. But it is precisely this type of occasion when Irving Graifman's heart aches the most. He cannot hold back the tears. He has a hard time attending large family events like weddings because, he says, "I never got to see any of my sisters get married."

With the exception of his brother, all of Irving Graifman's family was slaughtered during the Holocaust. Today, Graifman still bears the emotional and physical scars of his own five years in the concentration camps—Auschwitz, Buchenwald, Theresienstadt and Kawinkel. The tattoo on his arm is from Auschwitz. It reads A18986.

Irving Graifman was born in Grodzisk, Poland, in 1923. His father was a successful carpenter and contractor. He lived in a gentile area of Warsaw from 1935 to 1939. When the Nazis came to Warsaw, they forced Graifman and his family into the ghetto with other Jewish families. They lived in a dank basement apartment but were happy to get even that. Graifman was there for three months before the Nazis began shipping the people out of the ghetto in trains. When he was sixteen, Graifman was separated from most of his family, and he went with his brother Alex and father into the camps. It was the last time he would ever see his mother, sisters or other brothers again. His mother and other family members were executed shortly thereafter.

One of Irving Graifman's earliest memories from the concentration camps was an incident in which he was marked for execution. With all his family dead except for his brother, Graifman was in a labor camp working in a munitions shop when he contracted typhoid during the cold winter. He was running a fever of 105. The Germans put all those suffering from typhoid and other ailments into one barrack, Barrack 55. Graifman, then seventeen years old, recalls the day it was determined that all in Barrack 55 would be executed. The Nazis began opening fire in the barrack as Graifman and others pleaded for their lives. When the shooting stopped, the surviving sixteen to twenty, including Graifman, were ordered out of the barrack and were marched down a hill in the snow in the middle of the night to face a man named Artur.

Artur, a guard who was working with the Nazis, stood about six foot six and was the most vicious person Graifman had ever known. It was Artur who on a daily basis was charged with executing people. On this cold winter night, Artur lined up the survivors of Barrack 55 in groups of four at the bottom of the hill. He then methodically shot them point blank in the back of the head as he shouted anti-Semitic epithets at them. By the time Artur reached Graifman, however, he had run out of ammunition. So he pulled out his pistol and placed the gun against the back of Graifman's head. Graifman was not sure what happened after that. He thinks he must have flinched at the last possible moment as the bullet, instead of entering his head, pierced his earlobe. Graifman fell bleeding to the ground and lay there, still, in the darkness of the night. As he lay on the ground, he looked up and saw his mother standing beside him. Yet he knew this could not be because she had already been killed. The image of his mother told him that everything would be all right from that point forward and that nothing would happen to him. More than fifty years later, Irving Graifman still weeps as he tells this story. It was a moment that gave him fortitude and the will to survive.

For Graifman, the botched execution and image of his mother were miracles. His fever went away and he never got sick again. At one point after this, he was forced to march naked for three miles in a snowstorm to get deloused. He did not get sick. For years he witnessed the slaughtering of his countrymen and other Jews and was repeatedly forced to watch other Jews being hanged or shot. He saw the Nazis take small babies and smash their skulls on the pavement and throw children off tall buildings. When those in the camps were starving, he saw people cut up other people just to eat.

Graifman and his brother were still together toward the end of the war. He recalls that approaching Allied troops would cause them to be transferred to other concentration camps and they would be forced to march many miles at a time. During those marches, his brother became very ill and started to swell. Graifman believes he was about 90 percent dead. He carried Alex on his back for miles and miles until they were separated by the guards. Alex was liberated by the Allies the very next day but Graifman had to march for three or four more weeks until he reached Theresienstadt in Czechoslovakia, where he was eventually liberated by the Russians in 1944.

Today, Graifman simply credits his own survival to fortitude. They would pray a lot in the camps, but "the will to live is very great." Graifman survived by eating any leaf he could find or any morsel of bread, no matter how bad. After a while, "when you see so much killing, you try not to think about it and you just go on."

After the war, Irving Graifman was reunited with Alex in a refugee camp run by the United Nations. He also met his wife, Ruth, another Holocaust survivor, and was married in Lodz, Poland. At the age of twenty-five, he and Ruth moved to the United States, settling in the Chicago area. Graifman had no money and little education as his schooling had been interrupted by the war. But he did have some of the carpentry skills that were passed down to him by his father. For years, he worked hard as a carpenter, saving enough money to start his own successful business. He now notes with pride the many houses, apartments and churches he has built over the years. His son has followed in his footsteps. "I can be proud that I contributed to my community. I didn't cost Uncle Sam one penny!"

In the mid-1980s, Graifman and his wife moved to Florida. As president of the Holocaust Survivors of South Florida, a group of fifteen hundred survivors, he speaks to young children in schools about his experiences in the concentration camps. "The children should know what happened," he says. "It shouldn't occur anymore but it is happening in Bosnia right now. We have not learned." The survivor group also sponsors a two-day event in South Florida every year for more than five hundred children. The youngsters are set up in groups of ten with a survivor for each group. They discuss the Holocaust and write essays about what they have heard and seen. He tells the children to stand up against people who are prejudiced, people who make racial and ethnic slurs. His lesson to them is simple: "One man can make a difference."

Irving Graifman's own life has been one of survival. To be in the concentration camps for that long and to live to tell the story is a feat in and of itself. When asked to define the essence of strong character, it is fortitude to which Graifman always returns. "What can I say? I lost my parents, my sisters and three brothers. But you have to live," he says. "You cannot bury yourself." Even today, Graifman still demonstrates the fortitude that got him through the camps. He goes on each day with the pain and the memories from years gone by, showing us what it means to have the strength of mind that enables one to bear daily adversity.

# Pedro Negrin: Working Toward the American Dream

*Sarasota, Florida*

*We often forget that work itself is a virtue. We learn by hard work what it means to earn something through earnest effort, whether it is a good grade, a job promotion or the satisfaction of knowing you have done the best you can do. Some of our country's greatest success stories are not the Horatio Alger rags to riches types. They are the people who work and work and work just to be able to afford the simple gifts in life: a home, a garden, a future for their children.*

Pedro Negrin works hard. He has had to work hard his whole life. Since coming to America in 1987, he has held two, sometimes three jobs at a time to support his family. Often, his multiple jobs leave him only two or three hours' sleep a night. Yet for all of this hard work, Pedro Negrin does not live in a big house, he does not wear designer clothing or dine at nice restaurants. Pedro Negrin is just doing what he understands living in America is all about.

When Negrin was fifteen years old growing up in Havana, Cuba, in 1959, his home was for many a tropical paradise. Havana was a city of sophistication, nightclubs, hotels and Las Vegas-style entertainment. But life in Havana was about to radically change.

In 1959, Fidel Castro took over and the Cuban people were generally optimistic. Castro was the conqueror of a dictator and was popular among most Cubans. However, shortly after assuming the reins of power, Castro began imprisoning and executing many innocent people. Negrin's Catholic church and school were shut down. Priests fled Cuba or went into hiding. Catholics, forbidden in any way from celebrating mass, huddled together in silence in their homes as a form of worship. At Negrin's parochial high school, the curriculum changed from that of God and Church to Fidel and the revolution. The students were indoctrinated with Communist teachings and compelled to pledge their allegiance to the revolution. Negrin never pledged his allegiance.

After his schooling, he went to work at his father's successful family-owned plate-glass company. The success was short-lived. The government instructed Negrin's family to prepare for a takeover of the business. Twice during this time, their home was entered by government agents, the family interrogated, his possessions searched.

After the government assumed control of the family business, Negrin was no longer free to choose his line of work. So for more than twenty years, he moved from job to job at the government's fancy. He married, had children and then separated from his wife. The government first installed him in an auto repair shop where he was trained by and worked for the government. Then he was transferred from this job to driving a taxicab for the government. Negrin said, "They controlled your life, your family, your mind." Frustrated with this type of existence, he applied for an American visa at the time of the Mariel boat lift, but the Cuban government prevented his departure. Desperately wanting to get his new wife and their small child out of Cuba, he applied for a visa to Spain, where his family had relatives. The government informed Negrin that although the house he owned in Cuba was completely paid for, the government's price for leaving the island would be the original price of the home. Driven by his desire for freedom, Negrin worked to repay the government for the house. The government then seized his home, his car, his furniture and his bank accounts.

Arriving in Spain in 1987, the Negrins moved to a town named Córdoba. For days the family slept homeless and jobless in a car. After much searching, Negrin approached a construction site for a job where he was promised only one day's work. He worked as hard as he could so that he would be asked back for a second day. Forty-three-year-old Negrin filled wheelbarrows with dirt and concrete in the basement of the building and wheeled them to the top floor for delivery. He did this for twelve straight hours. Back and forth, back and forth. To his relief, Negrin was invited back for another "conditional" day of work. Again, he filled and pushed the wheelbarrow for four days straight until he was offered a permanent position as a laborer. All day long, he worked in the hot sun while at night he cleaned office buildings. He was still barely making enough money to afford a tiny apartment.

By the end of the year, the Negrins obtained U.S. visas. They moved to Florida in December 1987 and located in Sarasota to be near family members.

Negrin soon landed his first job with a cleaning company. He and his wife worked at cleaning office buildings both day and night. For their first two years in this country, they worked a grueling amount of hours just to survive. The cleaning shift for them went from 5:00 P.M. until 2:00 or 3:00 A.M. They were living on only two to three hours of sleep each night, working seven days a week. After two years, Negrin found new employment that reduced the amount of hours he was working each day, but not by much. He began work as a daytime janitor at a Sarasota hospital, and his shift went from 7:00 A.M. to 3:30 P.M. Then Negrin would put on his cleaning gear and clean office buildings from 5:00 P.M. to 4:00 A.M. As a result of such dedication, the Negrins were able to save enough money for a down payment on a house.

Pedro Negrin still works at a pace most of us would

consider backbreaking. This year, the hospital presented him with a pen normally reserved for those who have worked at least fifteen years. The hospital determined that Negrin was worthy of this token of appreciation nine years ahead of schedule. For in his six years of work at the hospital, Negrin has never missed a day of work, has never called in sick, has never been late, has never taken time off. It is a streak that Cal Ripken, Jr., would marvel at.

Negrin thinks he has it good because he now has weekends off. However, most of these weekends are spent working on the house or working for neighbors to make some extra money. During the work week, the days continue to be amazingly long. He works at the hospital from 7:00 in the morning until 3:30 P.M. and cleans offices from 6:00 P.M. until midnight. He says that he never considered taking welfare in any form. Negrin has always been a firm believer in hard work, no matter what form it takes. Although, he says, "I don't want my son to have to work as hard as I do." That is why Pedro Negrin is working so hard now.

Negrin and his family became U.S. citizens in the summer of 1995. What does this new citizenship mean to Negrin? "This is home now.... In the United States, you can be free, you can choose your job, you can buy a house, you can shop in stores ... and you can vote!"

The year 1996 will be special for Negrin and his wife. For the first time in their lives, they will join other Americans and cast their vote in free, democratic elections—a right Pedro Negrin has definitely earned through the virtue of hard work.

# Doug Smith:
# Building Men of Integrity on the River

## *Jacksonville, Florida*

*In many of our profile stories, we have heard "character" defined as making the right choices in life. In Jacksonville, there is a program called Safe Harbor Boys Home whose motto is: "Learning to choose the right course for life." It is run by a man named Doug Smith and his wife, Robbie. Smith's own life story is one of destitution and recovery. In a most unlikely scenario, Smith now finds himself living a life on the water, teaching character to many of our modern-day Huckleberry Finns. Today, he can boast of a success rate with these boys of better than 90 percent. Strict discipline and an understanding of the virtue of personal responsibility has made all the difference in the lives of these young men. Where others have failed, Doug Smith continues to succeed.*

At the age of twelve, Doug Smith was homeless and roaming the riverfront of Jacksonville. He was without direction, purpose or supervision.

When Smith was two years old, his father died in a car accident and his mother remarried a man who Smith says was an abusive schizophrenic. At home, Smith would receive whippings every day—mostly because he could not read. He suffered from dyslexia. When his stepfather asked him to read something and he couldn't, the beatings would commence. One day Smith just left.

Living underneath the Trout River Bridge, he would work with local shrimpers, who paid him one pound of shrimp a day. He would then take the shrimp to a seafood restaurant and trade it in for a meal. At night under the bridge, he would sleep with a stray dog, a German shepherd he befriended.

It was against the law at that time to be homeless, so Smith says he was arrested a lot. On one Christmas day, alone with his dog, Smith was sitting on a street curb eating a hamburger when a police officer approached him. The officer told Smith they would have to move, but Smith refused. After some words, the officer shot and killed Smith's dog. Smith was arrested. He found himself in juvenile detention for three months. Despair set in. Smith thought he would never get out. There were few foster parents who were looking to take on the responsibility of a teenager, and, besides, he was told by officials there was a waiting list of ten other boys ahead of him who were waiting for foster parents. He despised living in the institution. The loneliness and confinement were too much. One night in his room, he tried to hang himself.

But Smith was able to put his life back together. He says today, "The past is the past. If you worry about it, you are a slave to it." Soon after the attempted suicide, with the help of some of his old bosses, the Seafarer's International Union offered Smith a scholarship to put him through a maritime academy, the Harry Lundeberg School of Seamanship, in Piney Point, Maryland. The union was even willing to pay for his clothes. After this schooling and working at sea for a number of years as a merchant marine, Smith returned to Jacksonville to work in the shipyards.

It was during this time that he met his wife of twenty-two years, Robbie, who turned out to be a significant stabilizing influence in his life. Together, they found success in a machine shop Smith opened in Daytona Beach. He made good money by making parts for the federal government. But the daily stresses of running a business of 150 employees became too much for Smith. He sold the shop for a large sum of money in 1982 and hit early retirement to spend more time with his wife relaxing on a boat they had purchased on the St. John's River.

The retirement would be short-lived. In that same year, a federal judge in Jacksonville, who knew Smith had volunteered to help the Sea Scouts, contacted him to request that he care for two delinquent kids on an interim basis for approximately three months. The children had committed crimes and were in need of stable housing. At first, he did not want to take on this responsibility and was bitter about being asked. For Smith, it meant reliving all the bad memories he had of his youth in the streets escaping a broken home. Said Smith, "The street is a very ugly place and you forget a lot of things; you have to." But Smith's own sense of responsibility took over. He and Robbie reluctantly accepted the challenge on the grounds that discipline, responsibility and Christian faith would be the cornerstone of this short-term foster care. More than one decade and 140 children later, these are still the principles guiding Safe Harbor Boys Home.

The success of Safe Harbor has been hard earned. Initially, in the 1980s the Smiths collaborated with the Florida Department of Health and Rehabilitative Services. Although funding was available through the department, the Smiths ceased their affiliation with the governmental agency when they learned that enormous strings were attached to the funding. Smith says that

HRS required them to have a smoking section for children and that fire inspections by the Coast Guard were not acceptable for the department. Furthermore, HRS would not permit the Smiths to condone homosexuality among the boys. Faced with continual paperwork and unreasonable regulations, the Smiths decided to completely forgo state grants and strike out on their own. Their funding was revoked and their license pulled. But Safe Harbor soon found alternative licensing through the Florida Association of Christian Child Care Agencies.

Today, the program is economically self-sufficient and the Smiths direct Safe Harbor in a volunteer capacity. Funding comes from private donations including individual contributions, churches, Sunday school classes, civic and social clubs. No city, state or federal dollars are received. And ironically, the Department of Health and Rehabilitative Services recently petitioned the state to have Safe Harbor assist in an adoption program because Smith has had a higher success rate than the state-run delinquency programs. There is now a waiting list of about five hundred for Safe Harbor.

Doug Smith's Safe Harbor foster care program cares for approximately twelve troubled boys at any one time. The boys, ages fifteen to seventeen, come to him from broken homes and many are usually carrying juvenile criminal records with them. These boys are tough. Many did drugs. Some are victims of incest. One tried to kill his own parents by running them over in his car when he was just eleven years old. The boys are usually referred to Safe Harbor by courts, agencies, churches or private homes. They stay for an average of eighteen months and then either return home to their families or set out on their own to get an education or find work. Many of the young men are victims of abuse and neglect. For these boys, there just aren't any families to return to.

The Safe Harbor "home" is a three-story, seventy-five-foot renovated vessel called *The Spike* donated by the U.S. Coast Guard. Many other smaller vessels have been donated as well. It is on these vessels that the boys learn about the water, marine life, boating, carpentry and fishing. The water is a calming agent for these rowdy young men.

But it is not only the river life that makes Safe Harbor unique. It is also the way Smith is able to teach the boys responsibility through discipline that is important. There is a point system that is merit based. Smith believes it is this reward system that teaches them self-discipline and how to make the right decisions. When a boy comes to Safe Harbor, he has no points, no privileges whatsoever. He cannot talk to friends; he cannot wear whatever clothes he likes. He is dressed in a uniform and then assigned chores. Everyone has a job that is essential to the welfare of all, whether it is cooking or cleaning or repairing the many boats. A ledger is kept that logs in positive acts by the boys. As months go by and responsibilities increase, a boy can build up his points and redeem them for certain privileges, such as going to the movies or out on a date or wearing casual clothing. The boys keep their own cards that list positive points and negative points.

The average workday for these boys begins at 6:00 A.M. Schooling takes place at each boy's own pace, but all are required to earn their high school equivalency diplomas while on board. The education component is provided by Robbie Smith and volunteers in a home-schooling atmosphere. Bible study is also a constant, as is community service. Every day the boys are voluntarily instructed from the Book of Proverbs in the Bible.

When the boys leave Safe Harbor for good, Smith hopes they will leave with one thing: integrity. He advises the young people, "Money will come and go but they can't take your integrity away from you. As long as you have your integrity, you can always make money." Smith has chosen to use the river and responsibility to build integrity in these young men, to teach them the lesson in character that he never had as a boy. Even today, it is an unusual situation for Smith. "I'm just an engineer who doesn't know a whole lot about kids. I guess I am the least likely person in the world to do this sort of thing." But that might just be the reason he has been so successful.

# Barbara Rowe: Picking Up the Pieces

## Maitland, Florida

*Often character is defined not so much by the things we set out to do as it is by the way we are able to turn adversity and personal catastrophe into something positive. Rodrigo Martin, a young friend of ours who was helping us research this book and who recently passed away after a courageous battle with cancer, once said, "When life gives you lemons, you make lemonade." The following story about Barbara Rowe personifies this statement. It is a story about faith and perseverance and sustaining the will to go forward and make a difference.*

Many people in the Orlando area recognize Barbara Rowe for her tireless commitment to public safety. As president of the Orange County chapter of Stop Turning Out Prisoners (STOP), she is on a constant crusade to keep violent criminals behind bars, serving their full sentences. She is also STOP's statewide vice chairman. This distinguished woman spends most of her time these days speaking before city council meetings and victims' rights groups. But few realize that Barbara Rowe's own life experiences have made her qualified to lead any number of organizations that combat social ills.

Barbara Rowe's story is one of personal tragedy and the constant struggle to put the pieces of her life back together. It has been a life checkered with premature death, yet the experiences have made her strong.

Born in Birmingham, Alabama, Rowe was adopted by a family when she was six months old. Her parents were loving and supportive, but when she was twelve years old, her father died very suddenly. This was followed by her grandfather's death when she was thirteen. And then, at age fourteen, her mother abruptly passed away. Barbara Rowe was all alone in the world. She remembers the moment she realized that she would have to become a survivor. Shortly after her mother passed away, a school friend of hers came to her house. He was crying and said to her, "Do not worry. Your mother is walking on the streets of gold in heaven. But what about you? What are you going to do?" She thought about it and, remembering the love and confidence her parents shared with her, realized that her faith would get her through this.

Two years later, searching for some stability in her life, sixteen-year-old Barbara married Charles Rowe, a real estate developer. Charles was everything. He was a husband, a father and a friend. They had two sons, Jeff and Chuck. In 1979, as real estate began to boom in Florida, they moved to Orlando to take advantage of a new and growing market. However, a recession soon diminished real estate market activity and Charles was forced to enter a new line of work. He opened up a pawnshop near their home in Maitland. The Rowes grew to love the community and made many friends. For years, the business prospered. Then one night, Charles and sixteen-year-old Jeff had an argument at the pawnshop. Jeff stormed out. Charles would never see his son alive again. Later that night, Jeff was killed by a drunk driver in a car accident near the Rowes' home.

Charles was terribly despondent over his son's death and threw himself into his work. He spent many a late night at the pawnshop. As Charles was closing down his shop one evening, two men approached the door. Rowe recognized one of the men, who had been a customer in the store earlier in the day. So he let them in.

The two men, ages twenty and twenty-two, robbed Charles, and then realizing that he could identify them, coldly murdered him.

In a short span of time, Rowe had lost her one guiding light, her loving husband of thirty-two years, and a son. But shortly after Charles's murder, tragedy struck one more time when her last remaining family member, her son Chuck, was stricken with the HIV virus. As Rowe mourned the loss of her son Jeff and her husband, she had to watch helplessly as this ravaging disease slowly took Chuck's life. In 1993, Chuck slipped away. It was nearly one year after Charles was killed. Barbara Rowe was now all alone for the second time in her life.

In the aftermath of such tragedy, she began searching for positives in her life. She came to rely on a number of close friends, who tried to keep her upbeat, and she turned once again to her inner strength based on faith to keep herself going. "I'm over the pain," she now says. "I'm angry, though, and probably will be for some time. They say passion drives creativity. In that case, I should be quite creative."

Right now, Rowe's passion and creativity have been devoted to leading the STOP organization in the Orlando area. Under her leadership and that of Kathleen Finnegan, the founder of STOP, Florida has seen significant progress in the laws governing prisoner sentencing. The next mission is to change the state constitution. Law enforcement officials and the state attorneys in Orange County marvel at Rowe's inner strength. She still lives in the house she shared with her family when they were alive. Her family now consists of two small Schnauzers, who keep her company. In addition to her work with STOP, she is the president of her neighborhood homeowners association. She is also busy attending college at Warner Southern College of Lake Wales. Someday, Rowe would like to help counsel children and families experiencing difficulties. She would like to pass on her gifts of perseverance and faith to others to give them some hope for their future.

Barbara Rowe knows how important a family is to the development of a child. She has had to experience the breakdown of two families in her lifetime. But the breakdowns of those families have never been by choice: Today, she sees the breakdown of families by choice: Mothers are not at home caring for their children, kids do not respect authority, government has taken too much power from the family.

Barbara Rowe believes that life is about what you do with the cards you are dealt. Clearly, she could have easily folded early on in life and become a bitter and unproductive person. However, she chose to rise above the pain and adversity. Rowe says, "Everyone has choices, and the ones we make determine whether we are going to make our community a better place or whether we are only going to care about ourselves and only want self-gain." Florida is fortunate that this remarkable woman opted to make a difference in the lives of so many others in our society.

# Clarence ("C.R.") Smith: Building Guardrails Through Faith

## West Orlando, Florida

*In* The Life and Death of King John, *William Shakespeare wrote, "Unthread the rude eye of rebellion, and welcome home again discarded faith." In central Florida, a once-prominent businessman has convinced gang members, juveniles, drug abusers and other coarsened members of the community to come off the streets to his Christian ministry and welcome home discarded faith. In almost thirty years as the head of Frontline Outreach, C. R. Smith has managed to change the direction in life for hundreds of youths. Smith is a character builder and a teacher of the virtue of faith—*

*faith in God, faith in yourself, faith in community, faith in whatever you believe in to make yourself a better person.*

Twenty-eight years ago, Clarence ("C.R.") Smith was leading the good life, or at least the good life for a man who grew up in the cotton fields of south Georgia. Smith's life was a local success story—that of a man who in 1951 as an unemployed veteran had to borrow $150 to start his first business. Years later Smith had lots of money in the bank. He owned and managed a number of appliance stores in central Florida that brought in more than $1 million in business. He had a house on a lake where he could water ski. He was able to buy his wife a new Cadillac and still managed to be a top donor at his church.

But by 1967, Smith felt as if he was missing something in his life. Says Smith, "There was a drive in my heart to do more."

For the most part, Smith had been a very devout man. He grew up in Ben Hill County, Georgia, the son of a man who was a heavy drinker and who worked on the infamous Georgia chain gangs for punishment for making moonshine. As a poor sharecropper's son, Smith would work in the cotton fields with the rest of his family. Smith says he learned right and wrong from his mother. Yet it was not until the age of sixteen that Smith attended his very first church service. During this service, with his cousins by his side, Smith was called to the altar by the pastor and asked to pray. He recalls a "certain peace that came into my heart" at that moment. Smith was so excited that he ran all the way home to tell his mother. From that point on, he was a regular on Sunday at the Lutheran church. Smith had found something called faith.

After serving in the army during World War II, Smith started a small business in Orlando but it was his strong faith that drove him to help Orlando's underprivileged and racially persecuted. In 1952, he opened the first over-the-counter credit business for blacks in Orlando. The move was unprecedented at this time in Florida and earned him the undying respect and admiration of the black community. Whites, however, were concerned and they let Smith know about it. But for years business thrived.

With a fourth appliance store in the works, Smith decided in 1967 that it was time to do more. He decided he would trade in his successful business and go directly to the less fortunate and the troublemakers in the Orlando community. Smith discussed his dream of a ministry with his wife, Estelle, who approved. Together they began to close down their appliance stores one by one. The Frontline Outreach ministry began in the back of one of Smith's delivery pickup trucks. With a bullhorn in hand, Smith would go into one of the poorer parts of town to meet blacks at his truck for Bible classes one night a week. Smith closed his last appliance store in 1975, devoting his life to Frontline ever since. Smith learned fast that the way to influence the lives of juveniles and street gang members is to build sincere relationships with them, which is what he did.

Between 1967 and 1970, every street gang in the Orlando area, roughly five in all, was dissolved, in part due to Smith's efforts. Smith says he was able to do this by winning their confidence and essentially "getting in their way." Because of his reputation in the black community as a generous businessman, the kids and their mothers looked up to Smith. When Smith would hear about some mischief that gang members were going to cause, he would find them and take them to the drugstore for sodas. He would stay with them all night as their shadow. Smith knew their mothers, and that counted for these kids. Many times, he found himself in the middle of a rumble, dodging bats and switchblades, with both gangs pleading to him to get out of the way so they could fight. Like Abraham Lincoln, C. R. Smith says the way to get rid of your enemies is to make them your friends.

It was during these early days of Frontline Outreach that Smith and Estelle adopted an abandoned black baby who was found sick and a young black teenager whose mother had died. These two children grew up in the Smith household with the Smiths' three other biological children.

Today, sixty-nine-year-old C. R. Smith has seen his dream of Frontline Outreach blossom into a multi-faceted ministry/community center. At the program's headquarters on Carter Street in west Orlando, Frontline offers a variety of services to the city's youths. There is food for the hungry, a day-care center for single mothers, teen pregnancy classes, after-school tutoring, high school equivalency diploma classes, crisis and marriage counseling, drug counseling, medical and legal services, as well as a pool, gymnasium and skating rink. Last year alone, Smith's program served more than 130,000 meals; provided more than 1800 food baskets to local families and free child care to more than 200 children; and counseled more than 1200 teen parents. All of this was accomplished through Smith's faith in Christ. Five thousand children and teenagers live within walking distance of Smith's ministry and he wishes he had the resources to help them all. He knows what ails these children. "Loneliness builds up inside them and then loneliness turns to anger." The Frontline Outreach center is a place where they are all welcome. It is a place where Smith teaches them faith in God, faith in themselves and faith in their community. Says Smith, "In and through the love of Christ, we are seeing takers become givers, losers become leaders, victims become victors and brothers' killers becoming their brothers' keepers."

Many gang members who came to Frontline Outreach are now doing productive things with their lives. Former gang members under Smith hold jobs or attend college and even medical school. Smith credits their changed lives to a renewed faith in God. He not only teaches faith to the kids but he actually uses faith to destroy whole gangs. "Changed lives in Christ don't carjack, become home invaders, kill or overfill already-crowded prisons. Changed lives in Christ become strong, productive citizens, builders of healthy families and taxpayers."

Smith hopes to muster all the faith he can for the days ahead. They could be rough. He sees so many children outside his front door in need of help, in need of character. And those in need are getting younger. He recalls speaking to a group of gang members about their conduct when one youth told him, "C.R., you think we are bad.... You just wait until these ten-, eleven- and twelve-year-old little kids get our age. You ain't seen nothing yet." Smith hopes to bring these little ones to Frontline to teach them how to live a life as "careful, mindful" persons.

This profile in character believes that "things won't change until people change." But he knows they can change. He has helped the worst of the worst to reform themselves. C. R. Smith talks about the importance of character—"that first cousin to conscience, that guardrail that keeps you going straight." It is C. R. Smith's job to build guardrails. For Florida's sake, he hopes he will have company soon.

# Epilogue

Somewhere, somebody hit it big—$1 million big—in a McDonald's peel-off game. But the winners Thursday were St. Jude Children's Research Hospital and its young cancer patients. The winner of the McDonald's Monopoly contest took a game piece worth $1 million, put it in a plain white envelope and mailed it anonymously to the Memphis hospital. St. Jude executive Richard Shadyac called it a "holiday miracle."

—Associated Press
*December 8, 1995*

# Notes

CHAPTER ONE: THE VALUE OF VIRTUE

1. John Marshall, *The Life of George Washington*, Vol. II (Philadelphia: James Crissy Publishing, 1832), p. 404.

2. Quote attributed to Alexis de Tocqueville by Dwight D. Eisenhower in his final campaign address in Boston, Massachusetts, on November 3, 1952 and as quoted in *Respectfully Quoted: A Dictionary of Quotations Requested from the Congressional Research Service*, ed. Suzy Platt (Washington, D.C.: U.S. Government Printing Office, 1989), p. 160.

3. Howard Fineman, "The Virtuecrats," *Newsweek*, June 14, 1994, p. 30.

4. V. O. Key, Jr., *Southern Politics in State and Nation* (Knoxville, Tn.: The University of Tennessee Press, 1949), p. 82.

5. American Legislative Exchange Council, "Report Card on American Education 1994: A State by State Analysis" (Washington, D.C.: American Legislative Exchange Council Foundation); The Annie E. Casey Foundation, "Kids Count Data Book, 1995" (Baltimore, Md.: The Annie E. Casey Foundation).

6. Roy P. Basler, *The Collected Works of Abraham Lincoln*, Vol. 2 (New Brunswick, N.J.: Rutgers University Press, 1953), pp. 220–21.

7. Elihu Root, *Experiments in Government and the Essentials of the Constitution* (Princeton, N.J.: Princeton University Press, 1913), pp. 13–14.

8. Aristotle, *The Nichomachean Ethics*, trans. David Ross (Oxford, England: Oxford University Press, 1991), p. 39.

9. James Q. Wilson, *On Character* (Washington, D.C.: The AEI Press, 1991), p. 5.

10. Aristotle, *op. cit.*, p. 29.

11. Tip O'Neill with Gary Hymel, *All Politics Is Local and Other Rules of the Game* (New York: Times Books, 1994), pp. 81–82.

12. Samuel K. Atchison, "It's Time to Start Giving Our Children Values," *St. Petersburg Times,* September 25, 1993, p. 3.

13. Alexis de Tocqueville, *Democracy in America,* ed. J. P. Mayer (New York: Harper & Row, 1969), p. 616.

14. William J. Bennett, "How to Teach Children Values," *Ladies' Home Journal,* September 1994, p. 142.

15. Gertrude Himmelfarb, *The De-Moralization of Society: From Victorian Virtues to Modern Values* (New York: Knopf, 1995), p. 242.

16. James Q. Wilson, *The Moral Sense* (New York: The Free Press, 1993), p. ix.

17. Daniel Patrick Moynihan, "Defining Deviancy Down," *The American Scholar,* Winter 1993, p. 17.

18. Benjamin Franklin, *The Complete Poor Richard's Almanacks,* Vol. II 1748–1758 (Barre, Mass.: Imprint Society Publishers, 1750), p. 92.

CHAPTER TWO: THE CHARACTER OF A CULTURE

1. *Jacobellis* v. *Ohio,* 378 U.S. 184, 197 (1964) (J. Stewart concurring).

2. Alexis de Tocqueville, *Democracy in America,* ed. J. P. Mayer (New York: Harper & Row, 1969), p. 525.

3. Ibid., p. 527.

4. Meg James, "Student Paid Hit Man to Save Career, Records Say," *The Palm Beach Post,* October 2, 1995, p. 4A.

5. Gibbons as quoted by Margaret Thatcher, "The Moral Foundations of Society," *Imprimus,* March 1995, p. 3.

6. Aristotle, *The Nichomachean Ethics*, trans. David Ross (Oxford, England: Oxford University Press, 1991), p. 104.

7. Michael Browning, "Walton County Spares Neither Rod Nor Child; Paddling Rate Is Highest in State," *The Miami Herald*, June 14, 1993, p. 1A.

8. Marvin Olasky, *The Tragedy of American Compassion* (Washington, D.C.: Regnery Gateway Publishing, 1992), pp. 167–68.

9. Ibid., pp. 182–83.

10. Burke as quoted in Tryon Edwards, *The New Dictionary of Thoughts* (New York: Standard Book Company, 1955), p. 686.

11. Mark Twain, *Following the Equator*, Vol. I (New York: Harper and Brothers, 1906), p. 264.

12. Mary Ann Glendon, *A Nation Under Lawyers* (New York: Farrar, Straus & Giroux, 1994), p. 227.

13. Sue Shellenbarger, "Bill Galston Tells the President: My Son Needs Me More," *The Wall Street Journal*, June 21, 1995, p. B1.

14. Robert Putnam, "Bowling Alone: America's Declining Social Capital," *Journal of Democracy*, January 1995, p. 70.

15. Tocqueville, *op. cit.*, p. 513.

16. Ibid.

17. Amy Waldman, "Lonely Hearts, Classy Dreams, Empty Wallets, Home Shopping Networks," *Washington Monthly*, June 1995, p. 10.

18. Charles Murray in his foreword to Olasky, *op. cit.*, p. xvi.

19. Clifford Stoll, *Silicon Snake Oil* (New York: Doubleday, 1995), p. 14.

20. Interview with Cliff Stoll, *NBC Nightly News*, June 22, 1995.

21. Judith Martin, "The Oldest Virtue," working paper (New York: Institute for American Values, October 1992), p. 3.

22. Peggy Noonan, *Life, Liberty and the Pursuit of Happiness* (New York: Random House, 1994), p. 70.

CHAPTER THREE: FOURTEEN DAYS IN MAY

1. Cheryl Ross, "1,000 Share Grief of Teen's Slaying," *St. Petersburg Times*, April 30, 1995, p. 1B.

2. Kit Troyer, "Somebody Stole a Friend of Mine," *St. Petersburg Times*, City Times section, May 10, 1995, p. 1.

3. Steve Rice, "Pastor Found Shot to Death in Her Closet," *The Miami Herald*, May 13, 1995, p. 2B.

4. Uniform Crime Report, Table 5, "Index of Crime, State, 1994" (Washington, D.C.: Federal Bureau of Investigation, 1994), pp. 68–78.

5. Ardy Friedberg, "Car Thefts a Runaway Problem," (Ft. Lauderdale) *Sun Sentinel*, January 27, 1994, p. 1B.

6. Colleen Mulcahy, "NAII Analyzes Costliest States for Auto Coverage," *National Underwriter, Property & Casualty/Risk & Benefits Management*, June 6, 1994, p. 7.

7. Virgil, *Vergil's Aeneid*, trans. J. W. Butler (Chicago: Wilcox & Follett Co., 1927), p. 132.

8. Grace Lim, "Teachers: Schools Lack Consistency in Discipline," *The Miami Herald*, November 16, 1995, p. B1.

9. Florida Department of Law Enforcement, "1994 Crime in Florida Report," March 27, 1995.

10. "Juvenile Crime Wave Coming, Feds Report," *The Miami Herald*, September 8, 1995, p. 1A.

11. Curtis Krueger, "Tough Girls, Tough Times," *St. Petersburg Times*, May 21, 1995, p. 1B.

12. National Center for Education Statistics, "Executive Summary of the NAEP 1992 Mathematics Report Card for the Nation and the States" (Washington, D.C.: U.S. Department of Education, 1992), pp. 9–10.

13. National Center for Education Statistics, "1994 NAEP Reading: A First Look" (Washington, D.C.: U.S. Department of Education, 1992), p. 23.

14. Keith Bradsher, "Low Ranking for Poor American Children," *The New York Times*, August 14, 1995, p. A9.

15. Carolyn Susman, "Top Students Cheat Too, Survey Finds," *Palm Beach Post*, November 23, 1994, p. 1D.

16. Wendy Weyden, "Teen Suicides Called Cause for Red Alert," *St. Petersburg Times*, January 24, 1988, p. 1.

17. Mary Jane Fine, "Why, Robert? Why?" *Palm Beach Post*, April 30, 1995, p. 1D.

18. Mike Oliver, "In Orlando, a Children's Dreamland, Why Do So Many Die from Abuse?" *The Orlando Sentinel*, April 3, 1994, p. A1.

19. Pete Mitchell, "State Ready to Crack Down on Elder Abuse; Legislators and Gov. Chiles Are Pushing for Tougher Laws to Protect Against Abuse of Older Citizens," *The Orlando Sentinel*, March 8, 1994, p. C1.

20. "Business Cases Clog Courts," *National Law Journal*, August 7, 1995, p. C1.

21. "Trends in Auto Injury Claims," PR Newswire, February 27, 1995.

22. "Butterworth Blasts Lawsuit Lunacy," *The Miami Herald*, August 3, 1995, p. 5B.

23. Michelle Pollina McDonald, "State Boosts Efforts to End Workers' Comp Fraud," *Jacksonville Business Journal*, June 16, 1995, Sec. 1, p. 10.

24. Rick Barry, "Extremely Daring Blind Man Hits Foot; Couple Sues; School for Guide Dogs Faces Costly Defense," *Tampa Tribune*, August 7, 1995, Florida Metro section, p 1.

CHAPER FOUR: OUR LITTLE PLATOONS

1. Meri-Jo Borzilleri, "Evert Takes Her Place in the Hall of Fame," *The Miami Herald*, July 17, 1995, p. 1D.

2. Meri-Jo Borzilleri, "Evert's Day Is One for the Family," *The Miami Herald*, July 16, 1995, p. 3D.

3. Ibid.

4. Manny Garcia and Tony Pugh, "Shot Dead in Street: A

Destiny Fulfilled," *The Miami Herald*, July 16, 1995, p. 1B.

5. Ibid.

6. Manny Garcia and John O'Neill, "A Killer at 13, Shot Dead at 18," *The Miami Herald*, July 14, 1995, page B1.

7. David Blankenhorn, "Fatherless America," speech to Family Research Council's Family Briefings, Washington, D.C.: June 19, 1992.

8. Edmund Burke, *Reflections on the Revolution in France* (Baltimore, Md.: Penguin Books, 1790), p. 135.

9. *See* Robert A. Nisbet, *Quest for Community* (New York: Oxford University Press, 1953).

10. Gallup Poll, February 21, 1991.

11. Massachusetts Mutual, "American Family Values Study," June 20–27, 1989 (New York: Institute for American Values).

12. Bryanna Latoof, "Bay Area Ranks High in Single Parents," *St. Petersburg Times*, January 10, 1995, p. 1B.

13. Diane Hirth, "Pensacola Haunted by History of Violence in Abortion Debate," (Ft. Lauderdale) *Sun Sentinel*, July 23, 1995, p. 1A; Office of Vital Statistics, "Florida Vital Statistics Annual Report 1994" (Jacksonville, Fla.: Department of Health and Rehabilitative Services).

14. David Blankenhorn, *Fatherless America* (New York: Basic Books, 1995), p. 19.

15. Ibid., p. 2.

16. "The Impact of Father Absence and Family Breakdown on Crime and Social Stability" (Washington, D.C.: The Family Research Council, 1993), p. 1.

17. Ibid.

18. "Crime: In Florida and the Nation: A Symptom of Cultural Decay" (Tallahassee, Fla.: Florida TaxWatch, 1995), p. 7.

19. "You Do What You Have to Do," *The New York Times*, April 13, 1993, p. B6.

20. Mike Langberg, "Tracking Hackers: Experts Find Source in Adolescence," *The Miami Herald*, February 25, 1993, p. C1.

21. Blankenthorn, *Fatherless America*, p. 46.

22. U.S. Bureau of the Census, "We the American Children" (Washington, D.C.: U.S. Department of Commerce, September 1993), p. 14.

23. Blankenhorn, *Fatherless America*, pp. 32–42.

24. Alexis de Tocqueville, *Democracy in America*, ed. J. P. Mayer (New York: Harper & Row, 1969), p. 291.

25. Council on Families in America, "Marriage in America: A Report to the Nation," March 1995.

26. David Murray, "Poor Suffering Bastards," *Policy Review*, Spring 1994, p. 9.

27. Jennifer Steinhauer, "Cohabitation Is on the Rise, and Not Just for the Young," *The Miami Herald*, July 26, 1995, p. E1.

28. Ibid.

29. Thayer as quoted in Tryon Edwards, *The New Dictionary of Thoughts* (New York: Standard Books, 1955), p. 191.

30. Tocqueville, *op. cit.*, pp. 62–63.

31. Tom Fiedler, "The Challenge: Dizzying Change," *The Miami Herald*, July 23, 1995, p. 1A.

32. Robert Putnam, "Bowling Alone: America's Declining Social Capital," *Journal of Democracy*, January 1995, p. 66.

33. Ibid., p. 67.

34. Francis Fukuyama, *Trust: The Social Virtues & the Creation of Prosperity* (New York: The Free Press, 1995), p. 310.

35. James Patterson and Peter Kim, *The Day America Told the Truth* (New York: Prentice Hall, 1991), p. 171.

36. Fukuyama, *op. cit.*, p. 73.

37. Diane Cobb Hernandez, Letter to the Editor, *The Orlando Sentinel*, August 19, 1994, p. A19.

38. Gallup Poll, "Religious Membership," 1937–1994.

39. Putnam, *op. cit.*, p. 70.

40. Ibid.

41. Marvin Olasky, *The Tragedy of American Compassion* (Washington

D.C.: Regnery Gateway Publishing, 1992), p. 131.

42. Sallis Tisdale, "Good Soldiers," *The New Republic,* January 3, 1994, p. 26.

43. Gwendolyn Stewart, "Thrifty, Brave, Solvent," *The New York Times Magazine,* June 25, 1995, p. 18.

44. Lou Harris & Associates and the Boy Scouts of America, "The Values of Men and Boys in America," 1995, pp. 8–16.

45. John Locke, "Some Thoughts Concerning Education," Vol. IX, *The Works of John Locke* (London: T. Davidson, 1801), p. 28.

CHAPTER FIVE: ABDICATION: SURRENDERING SELF-GOVERNMENT

1. James Madison, *The Federalist,* No. 39, ed. Jacob Cooke (Franklin, Penn.: The Franklin Library, 1961), p. 269.

2. Cory Lancaster, "Parents Ask for Reform of HRS," (Ft. Lauderdale) *Sun Sentinel,* March 8, 1995, p. 16A.

3. Frank I. Luntz, "Americans Talk About the American Dream," in *The New Promise of American Life,* Lamar Alexander and Chester E. Finn, Jr. (Indianapolis, Ind.: The Hudson Institute, 1995), p. 62.

4. Thomas Carlyle, *Past and Present,* book 4, ed. Richard D. Altick, 1965, p. 267.

5. *Social spending* is measured by the authors as total appropriations to the Department of Health and Rehabilitative Services and the Agency for Health Care Administration. In the early 1960s, before the creation of these departments, social spending figures were calculated to include funds for public assistance programs in existence at that time, such as AFDC, old age assistance, aid to the blind, aid to the disabled and general assistance plus the administration costs of those programs.

6. *Budget Watch* (Tallahassee, Fla.: Florida TaxWatch, November 1994), p. 2.

7. "Education Revolution: Home Schooling, Charter Schools,

and School Choice," *The Ethnic Newswatch*, June 30, 1995, p. 6.

8. American Legislative Exchange Council, "Report Card on American Education 1994: A State by State Analysis" (Washington, D.C.: American Legislative Exchange Council Foundation), pp. 35–36.

9. Ibid., pp. 10 and 40.

10. Madison, *op. cit.*, No. 51, p. 373.

11. Dumas Malone, *Jefferson and His Time*, Vol. 4 (Boston: Little, Brown, 1970), p. 22.

12. Warren Richey and Stephanie Smith, "Felons Beat Their Rap Sheets: Multiple Crimes May Not Earn More—or Any—Time in Jail," (Ft. Lauderdale) *Sun Sentinel*, March 26, 1995, p. 1A; the Florida Sheriff's Association; the State Attorney's Office, Second Judicial Circuit.

13. Ibid.

14. Michael Browning, "Perspective on Paradise: The Needy," *The Miami Herald*, July 24, 1995, p. 1A.

15. The Annie E. Casey Foundation, "Kids Count Data Book, 1995" (Baltimore, Md.: The Annie E. Casey Foundation), p. 139.

CHAPTER SIX: THE PROFILES IN CHARACTER

1. Debbie Cenziper, "Experts: Vital Idols Missing, Youths Struggle to Name Heroes," (Ft. Lauderdale) *Sun Sentinel*, July 17, 1994, p. 1B.

2. Geoffrey C. Ward and Ken Burns, *Baseball: An Illustrated History* (New York: Knopf, 1994), p. 37.

3. Tom R. Wagy, *Governor LeRoy Collins, Spokesman of the New South* (Tuscaloosa, Ala.: The University of Alabama Press, 1985), p. 81.

4. Rick Edmonds, "The Push for Equality: Journey to the Selma Bridge," *Forum*, Winter 1994/1995, Florida Humanities Council, p. 33.

5. Wagy, *op. cit.*, pp. 80–81.

6. Ibid., pp. 88–89.

7. Ibid., pp. 135–36.

♻ Printed on Recycled Paper

# About the Authors

Jeb Bush is the president and chief operating officer of the Miami-based Codina Group and the chairman of the Foundation for Florida's Future, a nonprofit organization involved in Florida public policy. In 1994, Mr. Bush was the Republican nominee for governor of Florida. He has also served as Florida's secretary of commerce.

Brian Yablonski is the director of communications for the Foundation for Florida's Future. Mr. Yablonski is also a practicing attorney who previously worked in the White House as a personal staff assistant to President George Bush.